FINDING LARKSPUR

DAN NEEDLES

FINDING LARKSPUR

— A Return to Village Life —

 Douglas & McIntyre

Douglas & McIntyre (2013) Ltd.
P.O. Box 219, Madeira Park, BC, V0N 2H0
www.douglas-mcintyre.com

Edited by Meg Taylor
Cover art and illustrations by Wesley Bates
Text design by Dwayne Dobson

Printed and bound in Canada
Made from 100% recycled paper content

Douglas & McIntyre acknowledges the support of the Canada Council
for the Arts, the Government of Canada, and the Province of British Columbia
through the BC Arts Council.

Library and Archives Canada Cataloguing in Publication

Title: Finding Larkspur : a return to village life / Dan Needles.
Names: Needles, Dan, author.
Identifiers: Canadiana (print) 20230486754 | Canadiana (ebook) 20230486843 |
ISBN 9781771623704 (softcover) | ISBN 9781771623711 (EPUB)
Subjects: LCSH: Villages—Canada—Social life and customs—21st century. |
LCSH: Sociology, Rural—Canada. | LCSH: Villages—Canada—History.
Classification: LCC HT431 .N44 2023 | DDC 307.76/20971—dc23

To Dexter
Best doggone dog
in the East

Contents

࿎

A Return to Village Life: an Introduction

෬

Modern literature has not been kind to village life. For nearly two centuries small towns have been portrayed as insular places that need to be escaped. But anthropologists tell us that the human species has spent more than a hundred thousand years living in villages with fewer than two hundred people. These villages are where the oldest part of our brain, the limbic system, grew and adapted to become a sophisticated instrument for reading the emotions of other humans and figuring out how we might cooperate to find food, shelter and protection. By comparison, the frontal cortex, which helps us do our taxes, drive a car and download cat videos, is a very recent aftermarket addition, like a sunroof.

The village is where consciousness, the knowledge that we will die, is thought to have originated. And the village is where almost half the world's population still chooses to live.

My little farm community in southern Ontario abruptly stopped growing in the 1880s, after the farmers had chopped down all the trees and exhausted the soil with slash-and-burn agriculture. Subsequently, our major export was our children, who took the first available transport south to find work in the city or headed west to find new lives on the prairies. The number of residents of old Nottawasaga Township remained constant for well over a century.

Suddenly, things changed. In the past few years people have been quietly fleeing the city in droves. In 2021 growth in small-town Canada outpaced the growth of cities for the first time on record. This was partly due to stalled immigration during the pandemic, but it was also driven by people who discovered that working from home was something they could do anywhere.

My farm neighbourhood's population has increased by 40 percent, driving real estate values up and giving us our first taste of rush hour and occasional cases of road rage. Real estate booms and busts have come and gone here several times over the last fifty years, but they were fever dreams fuelled by waves of recreational buyers, weekenders and retired people and always came to a crashing halt with any hiccup in the economy. This current wave is proving to be very durable and the first to bring us young couples with children.

What to make of this sudden influx of city people? The clash of cultures is dramatic. The main street has been completely boutiqued and bistroed. In the old family diner the linoleum, Arborite and Pyrex have been replaced with chrome, steel and glass. An enormous Italian espresso machine has displaced the ancient grill. Wait times for hospital surgeries rival those for road construction projects. An army of officials enforces dog licences, burn permits, cycling and recycling habits and septic tank repairs. We have a dog park and an arboretum.

Older residents mutter darkly that the world they knew is turning into the cookie-cutter world of the city. But there are strong forces at work preventing that from happening. The small town is still very much a glass house. Eyes are everywhere. People who grew up enjoying the anonymity of the city find they must learn to account for their behaviour when they see the same people every day in the grocery aisle. Like many famous characters in Thomas Hardy's novels of rural Victorian England, they begin to feel pressure to lead a blameless life.

In these pages we'll take a walk through the Canadian village of the twenty-first century, observing customs and traditions that endure despite the best efforts of Twitter, Facebook and Amazon. We'll look at the buildings and organizations left from the old rural community, why they were built in the first place and how they have adapted to the modern day. The post office, the general store, the church, the school and the service club all remain standing, but they operate quite differently than they did for our ancestors. The farm calendar of planting and harvest may have faded from memory, but our speech is still peppered with references to crops and the weather.

Rural people are historically practical, tolerant, resourceful—and some find us dryly amusing—but we are also a fractious and disputatious people, slow to bless and quick to judge. We are divided by more than what unites us. We are townies or we are rural, we are professional or we are blue collar, we are seasonal or we are permanent. We tend to resist supervision, we suffer from low risk perception and we're very superstitious. The only thing we agree on is the big city. In this tour down the Seventh Line, we will look at what has changed, what is new and what is as eternal as the limestone cliffs that loom over the valley. In Canada, as seemingly everywhere in the world, the national conversation may be driven by urban voices, but the national character is often very much a product of small towns and back roads.

A Sense of Place,
a Sense of Purpose

৵

The land I live on used to be a farm. It's been in and out of crop production several times over the last four centuries. A group of Wendat farmers first migrated north from the shores of Lake Ontario in the late 1500s and started growing corn, beans, squash and a few small plots of tobacco. By 1649 they were growing enough to support a town of 5,000 people. That was when the Haude-nosaunee attacked, and the population scattered. The land returned to bush for two centuries. Farming eventually started up again in the 1830s when the first Jardine family moved down from their 5 acres on the hill in Duntroon to start clearing the trees off their 400-acre allotment along the sideroad that eventually carried their name. Within two generations the trees were all gone and the land exhausted. The township emptied out once again as most of the Jardines gave up farming and moved to the city or tried their luck in the Canadian West. The township dug in for a depression that lasted half a century. The postwar Green Revolution eventually brought these farms back to life, but only for cash croppers to grow corn, beans and wheat. The cattle herds and sheep flocks had long since disappeared, and the wire fences mouldered down into the hedgerows. I arrived in 1978 to find the old Jardine farmhouse dilapidated and abandoned and the 30-acre field planted in corn. The only other signs of life were the small plots of cannabis growing in the bush at the back of the farm. So not that much had changed in four hundred years.

The notion that farming is a full-time occupation would have mystified both the Wendats and the early Scottish settlers. Neither spent more than a few months growing and harvesting crops, and the work was spread out over the year. There was lots else to do, including hunting and fishing, picking fights with the neighbours and figuring out what to do for five months while the land lay under a thick blanket of snow.

I tried growing winter wheat on the field that first season, hiring a neighbour to work the field and harvest the crop in August. When I totted up the results there was no profit, and not even enough revenue to qualify for the property tax reduction. I decided to let the neighbour rent the field and leave farming to the professionals. The field has been rented for forty-three years now, and my own farming efforts have been restricted to the front 6 acres of pasture, garden and barns.

In the meantime the neighbourhood itself has changed from a place where things used to be grown and made into a place where people mostly come to relax, many of them permanently. All of the properties on the hill above us are now inhabited by urban folk who flee the smog every Friday night and curl up in front of their gas fireplaces to watch the sunset. The farmers and Collingwood shipyard workers have almost all retired to condos and nursing homes in town. Those few who still live on the sideroad have found new ways to make a living. The landscape is dotted with craft breweries, cideries, spas, yoga studios, rock climbing gyms—all offering diversion and comfort away from the sodium glare of the city. The neighbourhood is very busily becoming something completely different, but in some ways it remains oddly the same. It doesn't yet think like the city.

Our community is a complex mix of urban and rural, full-time and weekender, professional and working class, sensible people and idiots. We remain a fractious and disputatious tribe. The only thing we agree on is Toronto. It has been a fascinating place to observe and write about, as I have been doing for the past fifty years. I have never had to look more than 5 miles in any direction for inspiration.

I've often thought we should put up our own statue of liberty on the highway into town that says: "Give me your teeming huddled masses yearning to breathe free, de-stress, detoxify and declutter."

Our children bring their friends here to rest, to explore different ways of being and, most of all, to eat me out of house and home. I wish I had their talent for living in the moment, but I am too busy cooking and cleaning to find that moment.

We still grow lots of food here at the farm. Besides the small flock of sheep I have maintained for three decades, I also pasture a couple of steers every summer, and they are joined by free-range pigs in the barnyard and fifty meat chickens in movable huts in the orchard. My potatoes are chemical free, and my eggs are omega-3. But increasingly there are no takers for any of it. Every second person who shows up at the dinner table claims an allergy to whatever we serve. They are going through a "cleanse" of some kind, whether it's from sugar or gluten or oxidants. Spiritual cleansing is great, and I'd be happy to write out a list of negative things in my life and burn it ceremonially while someone bangs away on a Hang drum. But these juice cleanses give me a sugar high and attract a lot of fruit flies. I checked with my doctor about them, and he advised me that I already come equipped with two of the most efficient cleansers on the planet: my liver and my kidneys. No one has come up with a more efficient system than that. He did say I should get out and walk more.

"We are what we eat, Dad," says my eldest son. He is turning into a kale plant. I always thought kale was more of a roofing material than a food. I gave the lad his own raised bed in the garden and encouraged him to have at it, and it turns out the soil in my garden is just perfect for kale. Soon he had a 3-foot-high hedge of it, and we were eating kale salads, roasted kale, barbecued kale, kale sandwiches and kale ice cream. I assumed it would eventually bolt like a lettuce and go to seed, but kale doesn't do that. It keeps growing bigger and tougher and ever more bitter until the snow flies. When the leaves finally turned brown and died, I assumed we would then dig up the roots and boil them too. But no, thankfully, the roots are poisonous. And so we are cleansed of kale until May.

For a century before I arrived, this old farmhouse hosted a parade of smoker-drinker-carnivores who poured Paris green arsenic on their potato plants and thought cleansing of any kind was weakening. Some of them died in bed, but a lot more were killed by falling trees or kicked to death by horses. They had no special secret to eternal life, but sometimes I think they had more fun.

When you live in a place the rest of the world views as a retreat, where do you go for respite? We sometimes put the barn on self-feed for a couple of days, borrow an apartment in the city and drive south to soak up the smog. I mix a pitcher of martinis and order in Chinese with extra MSG. Then I run a hot bath and pour in a bag of oxidants, some gluten for the skin and a pinch of Roundup for overall health. After a couple of days of this I am re-toxified and ready to return to the countryside.

But bigger questions remain: How does a Renaissance man (or woman) make use of a small farm in the post-industrial age? There's certainly no money in it. Do these small plots still have a purpose, and if so, what would that be? And finally, the question that has preoccupied our species for a long time, the same one addressed by the ancient

Greeks in their theatres: How are we supposed to conduct ourselves in this strange new world we have created? By writing this book, I hope to nudge my way toward an answer to all three.

I've always felt like a bit of a rebel, living as I have for most of my adult life as a back-to-the-lander, filling the freezer every fall with food I produce myself on these 6 acres. The old farmers around me have always looked skyward in exasperation as they've watched me flail around with my twenty sheep and a menagerie of re-homed horses, dogs, donkeys and poultry. But to the bearded hobbits in my son's rock-climbing group, I am hopelessly mainstream and a slave to consumer culture.

I enjoy the company of the rock climbers nonetheless. Vegans, pacifists and herbalists no longer make me flinch the way they once did. I've come to agree with the poet William Blake, who said that the man who never changes his mind about anything becomes like standing water "and breeds reptiles of the mind."

Figuring out what to do with a farm property begins with new thinking. It's healthy for a person to do this. Science offers evidence that changing your mind is like aerobic exercise for the brain. Asking the neurons to find different pathways helps keep the synapses supple. According to the Mayo Clinic, rigid thinking leads to rigid everything else in the grey matter, and they recommend we change our minds about something as frequently as possible. This is not hard to do when you still have adult children living in the house.

One of these opportunities to view the world differently popped up a couple of summers ago when a barefoot climber emerged from his van to collect my son for a day on the limestone cliffs of the Niagara Escarpment. He had feet like a hobbit, leathery on the bottom and hairy on top. I took him over to the sheep barn and showed him my small flock of crossbred lambs, thinking he might be impressed with my efforts to feed the house from this little acreage.

He said bluntly that farming was a blight on the planet, a guzzler of fossil fuels and pretty much the source of most of our current problems. "Farming is the cause of social stratification, coercion, alienation and overpopulation," he said solemnly. "Humans did not raise armies until they started farming and had to defend their land. We would be better off without it." He sounded strangely like my Harvard-educated grandfather, Dr. Arthur Goulding, the Edwardian doomsayer of East York, speaking out of the mists of time from his 5 acres in what was then forest between Victoria Park Avenue and Dawes Road in the middle of Toronto. (I'll come back to him later.) He leaned back just as confidently on the cucumber frame of a worldview he had tacked together with the help of Robert Malthus, Karl Marx, Friedrich Nietzsche and Aldous Huxley.

"Right," I said. "It will not be long now, comrades. So what do you eat?"

He said he preferred wild food. He was a forager. He lived on mushrooms and forest greens, and he drank a lot of kombucha.

"Ah, the paleo diet," I said and started telling him about Dr. Goulding, the founding eccentric in our family, who invented his own paleo diet twenty years before *The Stone Age Diet* was published by a California gastroenterologist in 1975. I left out the part about him being a total nutbar, walking away from his practice as a pediatric ophthalmologist in his thirties and spending the last forty years of his life in the basement making birdhouses. He had a physical resemblance to this rock climber, somewhere between George Bernard Shaw and the Unabomber.

"So, this township is not a great place to forage between November and June," I said to the hobbit. "What do you eat then?"

He allowed that not all the food he finds is wild. Some of it comes from dumpsters behind grocery stores where tons of perfectly healthy vegetables are tossed because they don't meet the rigid standards of the fresh produce aisle. At my age dumpster diving is not recommended, and in a small town, eyes are everywhere.

I asked him what sort of work he did and learned that foraging is both a state of mind and a full-time occupation. The young man has explored every square foot of the escarpment and follows a rigid code of simplicity that would challenge a Trappist monk. He treads lightly on the earth and shuns invasive practices like hammering steel pitons into cracks in the rock. He is an ardent follower of the creed of "clean climbing," using only nuts and runners that leave no mark on the rock face. Yvon Chouinard, the billionaire founder of Patagonia, calls it "organic climbing for the natural man."

The conversation turned abruptly to politics. My hobbit friend classified himself as anarcho-primitivist. I told him that I generally wake up Conservative, but by nightfall I have become an anarchist myself. Anarchists are not the bomb-throwing crazies of my grandfather's era. The national anarchist party in Greece now occupies several floors of a downtown office tower in Athens. The hobbit smiled and agreed that just because you hate structure doesn't mean you have to be disorganized. We left the problem of what we are to do with this piece of ground unsolved, but we parted friends and, apart from the snaky business of dumpster diving, I felt that my mind was still relatively uncluttered by reptiles.

After four decades of watching someone else till my back field, I lunged at an offer from the Nottawasaga Conservation Authority and planted fifteen hundred trees to expand the hardwood bush at the back of the farm and restore the hedgerows. Over the season my wife noticed that the new trees got me out and walking over that part of the farm more often than at any other time since we were married. After being hectored by my doctor for ten years that I should get away from my desk, suddenly I was doing it. So this spring I have planted another four thousand trees. Then I sowed the rest of the farm down to hay and permanent pasture and started building new fences. The economics make no more sense than they did forty years ago or a hundred years ago. But anything that confuses an economist usually makes the community a better place to live.

Not the Best Place to Write a Novel

৯

When I bolted from the insurance company in the city to live here full time in 1988, the idea of a home office was not widely accepted. People had studies in their homes, but in those days employers scoffed at the notion you might do all your work from there. Wouldn't you spend all day in your pyjamas watching television?

My friends worried that my brain would atrophy without the stimulation of "people friction," and I would become unproductive. I assured them that if my brain didn't have to think about the life insurance business ever again, it would probably thrive. Besides, I argued, once you took the commuting and all those pointless meetings and business lunches out of your day, you gained a seven-hour time advantage over everyone else.

"Yes," they said. "I suppose you would have lots of time to think and write out there."

Well no, you don't, because other distractions swoop in to replace the old ones. I once tried writing a novel at my mother's farm, even though I already knew that a cabin in the woods in winter was a tricky place to concentrate on anything but survival. In 1974 I dropped out of school two credits short of an economics degree and took the train north to the Rosemont farm, imagining that the silence of the Canadian forest would help me think long uninterrupted thoughts and commit them to paper by the light of a candle while the wind sculpted snowdrifts around the house. Omar Sharif did this very well in *Doctor Zhivago*. He scribbled feverishly with a pen and inkwell in front of the fireplace late at night while Julie Christie slept and the wolves howled in the moonlit field in front of the dacha. There was a lot of crumpled paper on the floor, and the theme music would falter and you could see this was all very difficult for him. But then Julie Christie would appear at his shoulder in a lace nightgown with a mug of tea and the music would pick up again and you just knew something really great was going to happen.

My log cabin had an open fireplace that pulled every cubic foot of warm air out of the house and sent it straight up the chimney. The drafts came in through the cracks in the logs, making the cobwebs in the corners float up and hang on the air. I chopped wood and stoked the fire until the couch finally thawed out. Then cluster flies emerged from the logs in biblical numbers and buzzed around the lampshades. By the time I had finished swatting flies and chopping more wood, I was very hungry. The cycle of eating, chopping, napping, chopping, swatting, picking flies out of soup and scanning the horizon for human company took up quite a bit of a writer's working day. After two weeks of this I called a friend. We met at the airport and flew to a warm beach in Fort Lauderdale. I tried writing at the hotel bar, but that didn't work either.

The conclusion I came to was that writing in a cabin in the woods or anywhere else is not a good idea unless Julie Christie is there with you and thinks you are adorable. So I took a job in town as the editor of the local weekly newspaper and waited for her to show up.

Thirteen years later I found her. Oddly enough, Heath lived just two miles north of the log cabin, on a cattle farm along the Boyne River. If I'd been a walker I might have found her sooner. After a whirlwind courtship we got married and she moved in with me in my apartment in the city. I talked about a five-year plan that would get us both out of the city and back to my little farmhouse in the woods where I would get started on that novel. Six months later, Heath announced she was pregnant.

"Ah," I said. "Now we have to get to work on that five-year plan, because who wants to raise a child down here with smog and gridlock?" I gave my boss two months' notice. That was thirty-four winters ago, and we are still here. People friction followed us, because we have lots of neighbours. Add the friction of children, animals, machinery, appliances and weather and you have a recipe for endless distraction.

E.B. White once wrote that "to live in winter in New England is a full-time job." He lay awake in the mornings marshalling the problems and projects of the day, none of which included sitting at the typewriter. He chopped wood, fed chickens, thawed pipes and plotted the murder of a fox that had been raiding his henhouse. If he ever got time to sit at his desk it was often just to flip through seed and poultry catalogues and dream of gentle south winds and spring. White was the next best thing to a recluse. He and his wife, Katharine Angell, were dedicated hypochondriacs and would not leave the farm even when the White House called to award him the Presidential Medal of Freedom. At White's funeral his son Roger Angell, the *New Yorker* writer, said, "If my dad could have been here today, he wouldn't be here."

One of my editors, Peter Gredig, who farms and writes in Elgin County near St. Thomas, gave me wonderful advice many years ago. I was apologizing for stretching a deadline to the breaking point and made the excuse that I had been "goofing off in the barn."

"Dan," he chided me. "What you are doing in the barn is not goofing off. You are exercising physically and using another part of your brain. It helps make you a better writer. So never call it goofing off." My neighbour Hughie gave me similar advice and was always encouraging me to get out of the house and pollinate with the neighbours because that's where I took inspiration. To be of any use to anyone, a writer certainly needs peace and solitude, but he must also keep the habit of living in the world, not hiding away from it.

Foxes and Hedgehogs

ಇ

The ancient Greek poet Archilochus left a scrap of paper on his desk that somehow survived, got copied and was passed down all the way to the modern era. The fragment said: "The fox knows many things, but the hedgehog knows one big thing."

The poet's message may be fuzzy for those who have never met a hedgehog. It is a curious little animal that rolls itself up into a ball and exposes its sharp spines if it feels threatened. The rest of the time it waddles around eating any small creature that moves. The fox, on the other hand, is a wily and adaptable creature that uses keen observation and cunning to get whatever it wants.

The farmers I grew up with showed foxlike abilities to deal with whatever problem they encountered when they opened the barn door in the morning. When I learned there were two kinds of animals to be, I decided I would grow up to be a fox.

The philosopher Isaiah Berlin stumbled upon the Greek poet's observation and in a 1953 essay argued that people generally fall into two groups: the hedgehogs who rely on one simple, overarching idea for making sense of the world, and the foxes who look at each situation

17

as they meet it and make up their minds how to cope with it. He wrote the piece as a joke and was irritated when the world picked it up, made it popular and remembered it long after everything else he had written was forgotten.

When I was at university in the 1970s no smart person wanted to be labelled a hedgehog. We all wanted to be crafty foxes. But then the business management school decided that having one big idea and refusing to be distracted by details was actually a Very Good Thing. Suddenly everyone had to be a hedgehog. In the insurance industry I listened to one keynote conference speaker after another insist that we must focus on the one thing our organization was good at and concentrate on that alone. We were supposed to forget about diversification, get back to basics and find our "core competency."

The very same thing was happening to my farmer friends back home. With the Green Revolution, farmers converted to hedgehog thinking almost as enthusiastically as any other sector of the economy. The twenty-five crops of my childhood got winnowed down to corn, soy and winter wheat. Livestock operations were concentrated into specialized barns. Fences fell and hedgerows were bulldozed to make hundred-acre fields. Many farm kids were just as likely to grow up without seeing a chicken or a pig as any of their city cousins. Hedgehog thinking in North American agriculture built massive fortunes while the rest of the world was figuring out how to catch up.

But Mark Twain had some good advice for people who put all their eggs in one basket. "Watch that basket," he said. Stuff happens. Things change. Just because you are very good at one thing doesn't mean the rest of the world will always need or want your One Big Thing. This past year I've had several conversations with cash croppers who told me that 160 bushels of corn per acre simply does not pencil out at today's price or cost of production. One of them put his corn head away five years ago and hasn't pulled it out of the driveshed since.

In 2021 end-of-year stocks of everything rose to the highest levels we have ever seen, and the bank economists assured us nothing much would change in the future. Then the Russians invaded Ukraine, the breadbasket of Europe and Asia. The world of food production has been turned upside-down. What is a poor hedgehog to do?

Suddenly everyone I'm talking to has decided that a little diversification might be the Next Big Thing. My cash crop brother-in-law is now a full-time mechanic in his own shop and his son runs the town snowplow. What was once an unbroken strip of corn and soy fields along our highway to the village now sports a cider operation, three market gardens, a mushroom barn, a hops plantation and a rabbitry, as well as pottery sheds, a koi fish pond and a bed and breakfast.

Any attempt to pigeonhole our species will come up short because we are not hedgehogs or foxes, or even sheep for that matter. We are *Homo sapiens*, and our special gift is our ability to adapt when the world changes. What stops us from using this gift is our habit of living our way into cul-de-sacs and swamps.

The idea that some people think like a fox and others think like a hedgehog refers to two distinct ways of thinking about the world: one that tolerates nuance and another that fosters simplicity. There's value in both approaches, and the bottom line is that you need both voices in the room.

My eldest son, Hart, has developed a fascination with the complex web of life in the soil. He is a philosophy student who gave up the restaurant business in the city about five years ago and returned to the farm to take up a career as an arborist. He came to trees through rock climbing and mushrooms. He has never been a farmer or even a gardener, but he is interested in food, and that, combined with natural curiosity, takes him down a lot of interesting pathways.

I remember when he was eight years old and we were building a rabbit hutch together, Hart asked me, "Dad, was Napoleon a good guy or a bad guy?"

"That is the fundamental question about Napoleon," I replied, reminding myself to keep the answer simple. "He certainly did a lot of great things, but I don't think you would have wanted to be within 500 miles of him while he was doing them. It's not always wise to follow a great leader."

But my son is unsatisfied with simple answers. He wants to stare into the microscope and count all the tardigrades in a pinch of topsoil. This can be frustrating for the rest of us because when the ground is ready and the forecast is good, we don't have time to count bugs. We want simple rules to guide us, like "Plant early" and "Plant to moisture." And don't forget "Don't stand near the PTO shaft."

I love to take the world apart to try to make sense of it, but some days I just need a few simple sentences to guide me as I head out into the field. Hart wants to give me the whole encyclopedia of the soil food web and talk about the difference between bacterial action and fungal action. As I fire up the tractor and hook onto the seed drill, I would be satisfied to understand that the basic objective is to do what I can to improve aeration in the soil. We're both right, and we will probably do the correct thing if we keep talking to each other. I think this is at the heart of the foxes and hedgehogs analogy. The combination of both types of thinking will usually provide the wisdom to arrive at the right decision.

Hart is left-handed and a lateral thinker—not an ideal combination for handling dangerous equipment. I never had the nerve to put a chainsaw in his hands when he was a kid because they are built for right-handed linear thinkers, and he lacked situational awareness. I discouraged extreme sports. I even told him the Blue Mountain ski resort was closed. When he pointed to the sodium lights on the hills in the distance, I told him that they were growing hydroponic lettuce in greenhouses. He didn't learn to operate a chainsaw until he was twenty-seven, but now he is up in a tree 60 feet off the ground with a chainsaw every day. I was as astonished as anyone to watch him teach himself to think like a hedgehog the moment he strapped on his climbing harness and hardhat.

I am actually reassured to learn that old Archilochus wasn't a philosopher or a business guru. He was a traveller and a simple scribbler like me. Perhaps he had just learned that the price of poetry was no longer meeting the cost of production, and it was time for him to go home and start growing figs and olives behind the house. I hope things worked out for him.

In the end, there is only one clear distinction within any group of humans. There are those who divide the world into two groups and those who don't.

Life in the Fishbowl

৵

If you live in the country it is important to wave on all occasions. If you haven't seen a person for several months, you raise your arm over your head. If you haven't seen them for three days, you engage the arm at the elbow. If you already passed the person on the road twice today, you just raise a finger on the steering wheel. And if you are carrying something heavy through the yard, like a bag of dog kibble, you snap your head backwards. That'll do. But the wave is essential. Don't ever honk your horn at anyone in town, but if you forget yourself and honk without thinking, give a big three-month wave out the window and that should repair any damage.

You have to be careful what you say about people out here because they are all related. It doesn't mean they like each other all that much, but they do talk, and stuff gets around. My wife is descended from one of the first farm families of Proton Township, 15 miles to the southwest, which means she is related to everyone between Highway 9 and Georgian Bay. So I have to choose my company carefully when gossiping. People up here like gossiping as much as anyone else on the planet, but we use an analog system that is much more reliable than Facebook or Twitter. My social media listening posts are the Driveshed Coffee Club on the Tenth Line, D&L Variety in the village and the loading dock at Hamilton Bros. Farm Supply down in the Glen or BJS Farm Supply in Stayner. It is no longer possible to park window to window with a neighbour on Civility Bridge and visit, as the farmers have been doing since the pickup truck was invented. Now you must seek out one of the quieter blind lines, like the one I live on.

I went into our hospital for a routine colonoscopy quite a few years ago, and the experience was like one of those dreams performers have where they are onstage in front of an audience and not wearing any clothes. The difference was that this was really happening. The nurses moving around me would have made a quorum for a meeting of the Parents' Council at my kids' school. One of them, my wife's second cousin, leaned over and said in my ear, "Danny, will we be reading about this in *Harrowsmith* magazine?" And I thought, "Why not?" I have spun my web out of thinner thread than this.

Living in a glass house demands more of us than merely exercising caution when handling stones. When eyes are upon us there is considerable pressure to think and move cautiously. This is the reason places like the Jardine sideroad emptied out a hundred years ago. Sons and daughters fled to the city to escape the harsh glare of publicity on the sideroads. They did win some anonymity in the city and probably better wages, but they also had to give up a circle of people who knew them better than anyone else. It was a very hard choice.

I think about the harsh nicknames they have for each other—Flatface, Dummy, DryCry, the Beak and many others. And they like to classify whole families for various behavioural patterns: the Smiths are drinkers, the Browns are hot-tempered, the Whites are cheap. I know that when I was growing up in Rosemont my own family was classified as interesting but hare-brained. We all spent far too much time with books or practising sword fighting and never learned a practical skill.

This is still an Evil Eye culture. You don't praise a child to her face, a crop in the field or a fat steer. That kind of comment attracts hail and aphids and makes the steer drop dead at the feeder. If you have to say something interesting about an especially fine crop of soybeans stretching away to the horizon, you shake your head, stroke your chin and say, "My, my. I've never seen a crop that good get harvested." That'll make you fit right in at the diner.

Above all, you must accept that you are under surveillance by operatives far more efficient than the CIA or the Chinese government. Eyes are everywhere. The solution of course is to live a blameless life ... and if that is not possible, you'll just have to develop a thicker skin.

Naming the Farm

~

If you have finally found that little acreage you dreamed about, your first inclination will be to give the place a name. It's not easy to come up with a good name that will stick. Forget about anything to do with the wind—Windswept, Windsong, Windstone, Windwood—they're all taken.

There's an app for this. You just pick an adjective and a couple of nouns based on stuff you have around the farm. I have helped so many people with this problem, and the names have stuck. My neighbour Bob King bought a farm in Grey County and told me with great excitement that there must be over a hundred snapping turtles in the pond.

"I'm going to call it Snapping Turtle Farm," he said proudly.

"Bob," I said. "I'm thinking resale here. Have you seen anything else on the pond?"

He thought for a moment and remembered that he had seen a snowy egret ... once, flying over a farm about 5 miles south. Last I heard he was still calling it Snowy Egret Farm.

Oddly, I haven't had much luck with my own farm name. I grew masses of larkspur flowers in my mother's garden at the family farm in Rosemont, and I won second prize for them at the Beeton Fair in 1959. When I came to write the Wingfield Farm plays, I named the village in the centre of the township Larkspur. Larkspur prefers sandy soil, of which there is plenty in the hills of Mono, but when I moved up here to the Blind Line I found the soil was very heavy clay. Larkspur will not grow in clay. But that didn't stop me from writing Larkspur Farm on the side of the truck and painting pink and blue flowers all over it.

Then I drove some sheep over to the fairgrounds, and the loud-mouth guy at the gate informed me that wild larkspur is listed as a noxious weed in four provinces and is poisonous to cattle.

"Why would you call your farm that?" he demanded.

I told him it was my wife's idea, and I had always wanted to call it the Blind Line Cash and Cattle Company.

"But you don't have any cattle!" he snorted.

"What's that got to do with it? I don't have any cash either."

Here's the thing. You're not looking for relevance in a farm name. You're looking for thrill. It's helpful if there has been some grisly crime committed nearby. If you are thinking of registering your farm name as a corporation, forget it. Some horse person has beat you to it. Way back in the last century the police stopped my mother when she was driving the panel truck she used for moving pigs, poultry and children and told her the law required her to have her farm name and address displayed clearly on the door of the truck. She selected Haystack Farm and then discovered there were dozens of Haystack Farms. So she went to a Gaelic dictionary and came up with Stuc án Fhier, which literally means "hill of grass." She repainted the door, and the neighbours always said she was Stuck on Fear Farm.

My Uncle Fred had a country property too, but I don't remember it having a name. It did have an elaborate gatehouse with a shingled roof, radio-operated iron gates and a large wooden coat of arms sporting the motto *Pas de jambon vendredi*. As a security measure the gate was a failure because the CB radio on the township road grader opened the gates every time it went by.

But the whole naming effort is pointless because whatever clever name you dream up, the neighbours will continue to call it what they always have. All farms go by the name of the last farmer to die in the farmhouse. My mother's farm was called the Smith Place for the entire sixty-five years she owned it. My farm has been the Old Currie Place ever since James Currie expired in the master bedroom in 1965. Before that it was the Jardine Place, a reference to a pioneer who gave up the ghost in the log cabin that used to stand in the orchard down by the stream. Mr. Jardine never heard it called that because in his lifetime it was known as the Jesuit Farm, in tribute to a missionary who was clubbed to death by the Haudenosaunee at the back of the farm in 1649.

Someday, down at the diner in the village, someone will eventually refer to my property as the Old Needles Place, but I won't be around to hear it because I will have expired.

DECIDING YOUR WAY
TO A NEW LIVING

‌ॐ

Now that you have settled in and named the place, you are now embarked on a lifelong quest to find new ways to make money. You probably have plans to garden and maybe live off the land. And you're going to have a solar panel or two. But you will need some cash coming in, and you won't be the first person to ask the question, "What makes money in this township in the dead of winter?" Something weird happens to cash when it comes to the country. It just disappears.

My next-door neighbour Hughie McKee quit a successful tire business and bought a farm when he was thirty-five. He moved here the year before I did and became my best friend. Hughie ended up growing 5 acres of apples and selling them off the back of his truck at flea markets, which may sound a bit desperate, but he was one of the more successful apple growers in South Georgian Bay. At least he kept going when lots of the larger producers gave up and quit. I often went with him on his excursions to open-air markets around the county, to help.

Our first trip together was one of those beautiful fall days when the wind barely moves and the whole world has taken to the roads to absorb the colours and the last rays of sunshine. We went to the open-air Keady Market in the middle of Grey County, and Hughie put me in charge of selling pears and plums.

"So what kind of plums are these?" I asked.

"If the people look Italian, you say they're Italian plums. If they look German, you say German plums."

"I see … and if they aren't Italian or German, what do I say?"

"They're called Stanley plums, but nobody's ever heard of them."

A woman interrupted him. "Have these apples been sprayed?" she asked.

"Yes, ma'am," said Hughie. "About eleven times."

"Oh, I don't like my apples sprayed."

"Well, you better not buy any of these. I've eaten them all my life and they don't hurt me. But they might kill you."

The woman looked at him for a second, and she started to laugh. And she walked away with a half bushel of Honeycrisps.

I turned back to my post and found a man staring at the plums. He didn't look German or Italian.

"These are Stanley plums," I said helpfully.

"These plums have been stung," he said. "Look at the sting marks on them."

"Stung?" I asked. "I believe they were sprayed."

Hughie was at my side instantly. "You are absolutely correct. They do have sting marks on them. But I nailed the little buggers before they laid any eggs. Look here." He broke open a plum and showed it to the customer. "See? No worms." Then he popped half in his mouth and gave the customer the other half. The man munched for a minute, handed me ten dollars and walked away with a basket of plums.

Then a man stopped in front of Hughie and gave him a sour look. "My wife isn't very happy," he said.

"Really?" said Hughie. "My wife isn't very happy either. She walks around mad all day. Why do you suppose that is?"

"She's not very happy with *you*. She bought apples from you last year and they were no good."

"No!" said Hughie in astonishment. "What kind of apples did she get?"

"She got Russets. She said they tasted woody."

"She's right about that. That's what a Russet tastes like. Just like wood. You can't eat a Russet. I would have quit growing them years ago except people keep asking for them all the time. You tell your wife she is absolutely right. Russets are just about the worst apple there is."

That stumped the man. "So, what's a good apple?" he asked.

"Try a Cortland," Hughie said, handing him one. The man bit into it, nodded and pulled out a twenty-dollar bill. And he lugged away a bag of Cortlands. Hughie stuffed the bill in his shirt pocket and grinned at me like a pirate.

"The rule is Never Disagree with Them, But Don't Back Up an Inch."

After about three hours, I felt like I was qualified to work in a Turkish rug bazaar. I sat down on an apple crate for a rest. "This is really stressful," I said. "I don't know how you do this every day. Am I any help to you?"

"Not much," he said. "Why don't you get up in the back of the truck and pack some boxes?"

Hughie had a grade 10 education, but he was one of the most observant people I have ever known. He would talk for hours about the lunacy of the system, why things didn't work in agriculture and what needed to change before any of it would make sense again. He was very quotable, and his voice has been everywhere in my work for the last forty years.

"You can still make your own jam, Danny. But you pretty much have to make the jars too."

The story of how he and his family found their way to the tire business that still operates on Highway 24 under the name of a national franchise should be required reading for anyone taking a business degree. It started when Hughie's grandfather Sam (Paps) McKee went into Clarence Brock's hardware store in Nottawa in 1937 and overheard someone talking about an auction sale that was coming up soon on Sam's farm. This startled him because he had heard nothing about it. Back at home he discovered his father had taken out a loan against the farm some years before and because of the Depression hadn't been able to repay it. There was indeed going to be an auction, and the family would have to find somewhere else to live. By this time Sam's eldest son, Robert Henry, or R.H. as he was known, had begun making decisions for everybody. R.H. moved his young family into a little house with a long backyard in the village and built a shed for his father to live in. (His mother went across the road to live with her mother.) R.H. was married with two boys when this happened, and he was completely humiliated by the loss of the family farm. It meant asking his wife, who had a good education and was a qualified teacher, to turn her hand to menial labour. R.H. began raising chickens in his backyard, and he and his wife killed, plucked and cleaned hundreds of chickens every summer and took them over to Wasaga Beach to sell to the day trippers from Toronto. They did this for ten years until R.H. realized he had made enough money to buy back the home farm. The new owner, Norman Hapgood, added a small surcharge to what he had paid for the property to cover the expenses he had incurred building a bridge over the river and planting a new apple orchard. He signed the farm over to R.H. in 1947.

The story should have had a happy ending right there, but the problem was that in R.H.'s early years, Paps had never set much of an example as a farmer for his son to follow. His formative years as an adult had been totally absorbed by the backyard chicken business, which is a comparatively narrow field of food production. It was all he knew. So when he moved his family back to the home farm, R.H. ramped up chicken production, stuffing the barn with thousands of broilers and putting up pasture huts for them in the old apple orchard. Then he went to the city to find new customers. The McKee children, of which there were now three boys and a girl, my friend Hughie being the youngest, grew up lugging 5-gallon pails of grain and water up rickety ladders attached to the outside of the barn to feed the chickens. They grew to despise the birds, but they also lived with a healthy respect for their father's famously hot temper. They learned to rise early and search the barns for dead chickens so they could be disposed of before R.H. found them and worked himself into a temper for the rest of the day. The business went reasonably well until the fall of 1953 when American poultry producers started building intensive chicken barns in southwestern Ontario and the price of chicken suddenly dropped from thirty cents a pound to ten cents.

"Ten-cent chicken made no sense at all," recalled Hughie. "We sent the last load of freezer-burned chickens on the train to Storks on Queen Street West in Toronto and held our breath hoping the cheque would clear the bank."

It did, and a few nights later R.H. returned from the Toronto stockyards at Keele and St. Clair with the announcement that he had just bought fifty feeder cattle from Alberta. This came as a complete surprise to the boys because there were no fences of any kind on the farm or even a corral to hold them. And R.H was no cattleman.

"Oh, Father," said John, the oldest brother. "Where will we keep them?"

"All of you go back to the river and cut some willows and we'll make a corral for them," his father ordered.

John, Bob and little Hughie did as they were told, and they had a rough corral built around the barn by the time the new herd arrived at the railway station in the village. The neighbours turned out to help drive the animals down the Nottawa Sideroad to the farm and into the corral.

"Oh, Father," said John. "What will they eat?" His father pointed to the hayfield. "Put up an electric fence and they can pasture that field until the corn crop is harvested." The boys fenced 60 acres with posts and two strands of barbed wire and put a single strand of electric in the middle.

"Oh, Father," said John. "All of these cattle have horns, and twenty-five of them are bulls."

"Go next door and see Arnold Vancise. He'll have a set of dehorners and burdizzo clamps." John did that, and Bob, who had a mechanical streak, figured out a primitive head gate using a V-shaped manger in the barn and a long hardwood two-by-four that employed the principle of the lever and the nutcracker to trap each animal by the neck as it came in to eat. Father watched as the first set of horns came off and blood spurted across the manger onto his shirt.

"I shouldn't have to do this kind of work!" he shouted angrily. And he turned on his heel and left the boys to finish the job on their own.

The next day John let the cattle out into the hayfield and watched to see how they would behave around an electric fence. One of the heifers walked up to it, put her nose to the wire and jumped back. Then she walked right through the fence and the rest of the herd followed her into a 40-acre field of corn that was ready to be harvested.

It was a very wet year and there was no way of getting a machine into the field anyway, so John decided to leave the cattle there until he figured something out. That day the cattle ate their fill of corncobs and came back to the barn at dark to rest. As it turned out, they didn't need a fence of any kind. The cattle went to the cornfield each morning and came back every evening right through the winter until the end of

March. When the very last corncob in the field was eaten, the brothers and the neighbours drove the cattle back down the road to the village train station and shipped the cows to Toronto.

R.H. took the cheque from the stockyards and bought shares in Bell Telephone, and so began a new career as an investor. He never again returned to the barn or any form of livestock farming, and from then on he could always be found sitting on the veranda reading the *Globe and Mail* Report on Business.

"I went that whole six months thinking the cattle venture was a total disaster," remembers John. "When we finally got the cheque from the stockyards it turned out that between the corn and the cows, we had done all right. But I never once thought of repeating the experience."

The question of what to do with the farm reached a turning point that year when the old orchard, fuelled by five seasons of chicken droppings, suddenly burst into joyous bloom and produced a massive crop of McIntosh apples. The brothers picked apples that fall and trucked them around to the west end of the farm, which fronted Highway 24 leading into Collingwood.

"In one weekend," said Hughie, "we sold enough apples to buy a new Chevrolet car. What can you do over the weekend today, that's legal, that would let you buy a new car?"

That moment changed their lives. R.H. suddenly adopted a new mantra: "It's no hardship living on the highway." The next project he gave the boys was the construction of a roadside stand and a bridge over the river so that anything the farm produced could be taken straight to the highway. Soon there were gas pumps, a lunch counter and a garage where Bob could practise his mechanical skills. They built a motel to give R.H. something to do, which was odd considering R.H. was not that fond of the general public. Then Hughie started selling tires to farmers and truckers in 1962. By 1975 the motel and the lunch counter had long since closed and McKee Tire had become one of Collingwood's leading businesses. Hughie sold his share to his brothers in 1973 and a few years later bought 175 acres on the Jardine Sideroad right next door to the property I bought in 1978. Hughie stocked his barns with cattle, pigs and chickens and planted 5 acres of apple trees. After my one unsuccessful attempt in 1979 to make a profit growing winter wheat, he began renting the 25-acre field behind my house. He would become the very last farmer in the township to make a living off 200 acres without off-farm work.

R.H. offers a textbook case that talent, smarts and hard work are useful traits but often not the determining factors in the search for prosperity. The most important thing is to keep making decisions, even if they aren't particularly good ones. Decisions usually lead you to wherever you need to be. R.H. decided his way through chickens, cattle, apples, gas pumps, a lunch counter, a garage and on to tires until he had decided his way right out of farming altogether. It is ironic that Hughie, the one member of the family to land on the correct square of tires, eventually abandoned that idea and followed his heart back to the farm. He made a success of it because along the way around that wide circle he became a great salesman and learned to charge retail prices for everything he grew.

But Hughie was part of the last generation born to the farm. He knew how to weld, set a seed drill, repair a rupture on a weaner pig and make a baler tie. Those are all lost skills, and nobody coming out of the city can expect to catch up on these subjects using YouTube videos. We're all now like R.H., who missed the chance to pick up that skill set when he was young.

How sensible is it then to try and make any sort of living from a farm? Is it just a lifestyle thing, or should we seek a serious purpose in it? This is a question I struggled with for many years after we moved here.

My father once said to me, "You are now working in the theatre and you run a farm as well. Shouldn't you be doing something that makes money?"

I majored in economics at university, but I guess it didn't take. All it gave me was formal instruction in how to make incorrect predictions. My mother once said, "Some people wave their hands when they're trying to make a point. Dan draws a graph." Economists assume that if people have trouble staying awake through their presentations then they must be practising some form of science. In 1977 I went to work as a speechwriter in the Ontario treasurer's office and quickly discovered that no one in the building took economic forecasts seriously because they had been dead wrong every year for the previous decade. Economics can sometimes be helpful in explaining what happened, but it offers no guidance for predicting what *will* happen. You need tea leaves for that.

About ten years ago, Hughie was looking over my sheep flock one day when he shook his head and said, "You really fooled me, Danny. I thought you'd keep the sheep for a season or two at most and then give it up. But here you are twenty-five years later and you still have the sheep."

I still have sheep because I like them. And that helps explain why most people on the land practise any form of agriculture. As far as I can tell, affection is the only explanation.

I'm one of the few people who can stay awake during the soybean price outlook lecture that is the cornerstone of all the farm conferences that take place across Canada in mid-winter. In fact my job for a long time was to follow the bank economist after he had waded through all his charts and graphs and wake the crowd up again with a funny talk. I remember attending one of those sessions during the 2008 financial meltdown and being startled when the economist told the crowd that average net farm income in Canada had been a negative figure for the past ten years. The room was silent, and it was difficult to know what people were thinking. I remember very well what I was thinking. If agriculture produces no net income, then it follows that it produces no income tax either. And if it is not a source of tax revenue, why would a government listen to anything it has to say?

That year crop prices spiked, and suddenly farmers moved back into positive territory. But not by much. Average net income since then has never gone much above $5,000. In other words, for my entire adult life most farmers have had to rely on off-farm income to support their farming habit. This is why they all laugh when I say that sustainable farming means you have a job with the township road crew and a wife teaching school.

When farm leaders are confronted with these facts, they shrug and quibble about who we should call a farmer. They argue that "real farmers" are the cash croppers—intensive hog, chicken and dairy barns with millions invested in land, buildings and equipment. That number is far less than one percent of the population. And, they say, even if this tiny core group doesn't pay much in income tax, they do pay vast sums in property taxes and a hundred other fees gouged out of them by regulators. This is all true, but the vast majority of the 60,000 people in Ontario who call themselves farmers are still part-timers and hobbyists who plant modest acreages, keep a bit of livestock and sell into a local market. They farm for reasons that mystify an economist. But there are still good reasons to do it.

So don't fret about making the farm pay. Apparently, nobody else does. Why should you?

The secret to using a country property effectively is to figure out little tricks that work for you personally on that particular piece of ground. It may not happen for a long time. It takes seven years for an asparagus seed to reach maturity. A Lipizzaner horse spends seven years in training before it is ready to perform. They say that most writers take seven years to develop the habit of writing every day.

Functional Stupidity
and Farm Safety

࿔

When I was a young man I worked for eight years as the public affairs director for a large Canadian life insurance company. It was considered a very good job, a position that my predecessor had held for forty years. He called himself "the headwaiter to the management floor." There was a very old man in my department named Gordon who hobbled into the office every day to work on the company archives as a volunteer. Gordon won a Military Cross in 1917 for leading a field gun crew at Vimy Ridge, survived a gas attack and the loss of most of his friends. But he lived to become the chief actuary of the company and a highly respected member of the board of directors. One day he was looking over a speech I had written for the president, and he said to me, "You know, Dan, this is not a complicated business. You break even on the insurance and you make money on the investments. And you try not to mess things up. That's all we're asked to do. Every day I come into this building I ask myself, am I the person and is this the day that we'll mess it up?"

I'm now sitting on a farm two hours north of the city because I decided at the age of thirty-seven that it would be a mistake to assume that my job as a generalist in an insurance company was indeed safe. I had already caught several organizations at the top of their game and ridden them down into the turf. It seemed to me that the insurance company was on the same flight path and would soon mess things up. Too many people who were smarter and more skilled than me had already fallen victim to restructuring and been escorted to the street. I didn't see how a mere writer, armed only with a BA, was supposed to navigate the ruthless changes sweeping the financial services industry at the time.

So I announced my plan to become a freelance writer and move to the country. My colleagues at the office instantly formed two groups. The first asked, "What on earth are you thinking?" And the second asked, "Could I come too?"

Old Gordon died two years after I left the company. Five years later management converted the business to a stock company in a bold but flawed plan to "play with the big boys." Not surprisingly, one of the big boys immediately organized a hostile takeover, and Gordon's worst fears were realized. The oldest name in Canadian life insurance became a free-floating apex: the name still exists, but the rest of the pyramid underneath, including 3,000 employees and $7 billion in assets, melted away onto other corporate balance sheets in the space of a few weeks. It was just business.

There is a conversation going on right now in management circles about how human organizations so often lose their wits and blunder into disaster. Many of us react with nervous disbelief when we watch public and private institutions march off under the flag of the latest enthusiasm, whether it is cryptocurrencies or no-fail policies in schools. We wonder how any of these ideas got past the committee stage to became official policy and received wisdom. A Swedish academic has put his finger on this syndrome and given it a name: functional stupidity.

Mats Alvesson, in "A Stupidity-Based Theory of Organizations," argues that mobilizing smart people is only part of what an organization does well. To be completely successful, management must at some point discourage reflective thinking and the expression of doubt, because doubt creates friction and friction has a toxic effect on efficiency. So organizations work wonderfully if the thinking at the top of the pyramid is sound and everyone obediently works to a common purpose. But if that thinking is flawed, the organization runs the risk of sleepwalking over a cliff.

Human organizations are unique because they use collective resources and complex hierarchical structure to do extraordinary things, like map the human genome or send a man to the moon. Huge pyramidal hierarchies are exclusively human constructions and are found nowhere else in the natural world. The rest of nature is a vast web of self-organizing networks that, under the microscope, look a lot like the township road map, or the human brain, or the mycelial filaments of a mushroom, or the internet. No pyramids to be found.

The secret to the effectiveness of the hierarchy is to unite the organization in its sense of purpose and eliminate all niggling second thoughts. But squashing doubt also discourages reflection. Alvesson says that when organizations lose their reflective power to regulate their thinking, they always get into trouble, and he came up with the term "functional stupidity" to describe this phenomenon. American political leaders believed that if Vietnam fell to Communism, then all of Southeast Asia would follow. The domino theory was a fallacy, and lots of people knew it even then, but no one dared to challenge the thinking at the top. America blundered into a decade-long march of folly because of that faulty thinking. Stupidity management was also successful in getting large groups of smart people to agree with the notion that collateralized debt obligations were a real investment, a mistake that nearly wrecked the international banking system in the financial meltdown of 2008.

The one bright spot in Alvesson's study is his observation that functional stupidity occurs less often in organizations that make a tangible product. If a widget breaks, your customer will throw it back in your face, demand a replacement or refund and tell you to make a better widget. Organizations that deal with intangible services like branding or fashion are far more vulnerable to the perils of stupidity management.

Which brings me back to farming and occupations such as working in the woods or the mines. Falling trees and unstable rock formations encourage a person to be alert and cautious. Doubt is not handed to a farmer in a respectful memo or by a thoughtful committee member. Doubt comes when clouds of soybean aphids black out the windshield of the combine or when two minutes of hail ruin the year's apple crop. Doubt comes when a loose article of clothing catches an unguarded PTO shaft and leaves you standing naked apart from your socks and your hat. The solemn and ancient warning not to put all your eggs in one basket survives as a vivid metaphor today because it still conjures up a picture of something fragile that can be easily lost through carelessness or bad luck. Farmers who face weather, pests and volatile markets never have the luxury of taking anything for granted. Country people who live on private wells and septic tanks must keep an ear open for strange noises from the basement. You become like that neurotic farm dog next door—very good at letting everybody know what might happen.

It all seems dreadfully unfair when you think of the soft life enjoyed by a branding consultant or a hedge fund manager. But dealing with tangible things also makes the farmer, miner or forester stronger, nimbler and, in the long run, more likely to survive. That is, they will survive if they learn quickly just how many ways there are to kill yourself handling heavy machinery, moody livestock or falling trees.

Obviously, handling tangible products in big machines has not made farming immune to stupidity management. It is a system that has made food safer, cheaper and more abundant than at any other time in human history. But it comes with enormous costs that we often don't see. We have become accustomed to buying jam that is worth less than the jam jar. And then we throw away the jar. How stupid is that?

I was schooled in farm safety by a group of adopted uncles and grandfathers from Rosemont. Keith Brett's farm on the highest point in the township was the training ground for new recruits, and it was Keith who impressed on me the great variety of life-threatening situations a farmer might encounter in the average day. He was always a step behind me, whispering words of caution: "Don't walk behind that horse without speaking to it, Danny. Never turn your back on a ram. Never leave the tractor running on a slope. Could be fatal."

"Could be fatal" was the grace note for much of his advice. Choose the lowest gear your patience will tolerate and then use the next lowest one. Don't raise the loader any higher than your nose when you're moving over rough ground with a load. Never, ever touch the clutch on a hill. Could be fatal.

We all know that a body in motion tends to stay in motion until it hits a hard surface. Running a chainsaw over your head is like running with scissors. And just because you can lift thirty-seven times your weight if your pry-bar is long enough does not make it a good idea.

Working by yourself, as most farmers do, encourages innovation and creativity. But it also encourages impulsive behaviour. My younger son served for six years in the Princess Patricia's Infantry, and his sergeant called him the Good Idea Fairy. That was because the sergeant recognized that Matthew had grown up on a farm and was used to figuring things out by himself in the moment. Matt accepted the nickname as a compliment until he noticed that the sergeant often referred to the senior officers of the battalion as the Good Idea Fairies. Matt eventually found a quiet moment to probe his boss's thinking on the subject, and the sergeant explained the Peltzman effect to him.

Dr. Sam Peltzman was an economist at University of Chicago who did extensive research into safety features on automobiles and their ultimate effect on injury and fatality statistics and was surprised that these measures had no significant effect on fatality rates. In a 1975 article in the *Journal of Political Economy,* he argued that each of us has a certain comfort level with risk and we automatically adjust our behaviour (usually in the wrong direction) if we are made to feel safer. Hockey players with helmets and faceguards just hit each other harder. Skiers ski faster with better equipment. You make a thing safer and then some people automatically push that thing until they are back in their comfort zone, and that is often not a good place. A driver who finds that anti-lock brakes will stop his car in half the time and distance he needed for conventional brakes will now drive twice as fast and follow the vehicle in front of him twice as close. He is no safer than he was to start with. It is a known fact in skydiving … the safer the gear, the more chances skydivers will take, in order to keep the fatality rate constant.

This makes farm safety people tear their hair out. They go to a lot of effort drawing pictures on lawnmowers and farm machinery—stick figures doing really stupid things with their machines—and they paste these pictures on the dashboards and fenders. Do the pictures help? The answer is, and always will be, not one little bit. In fact some of the pictures look like fun. Who knew you could play catch with your front-end loader? I have captured this type of human behaviour in a mathematical equation: Safety Choices = Effort Saved × Bragging Rights ÷ Probability of Public Humiliation.

I see Matthew go by on the riding mower. He leans down to grab a twig off the lawn, one toe in the steering wheel and one hand on the seat to keep the safety shut-off switch from activating. In that brief moment you can see that human progress is really nothing more than a series of bar bets. "If I can do that, then why can't I do this? Here, hold my beer."

His mother, watching from the veranda says, "He'll be fine ... if he's allowed to live."

At least we don't have to deal with any deadly species in this country. Australia has at least thirty of the world's most dangerous creatures, including snakes and spiders on land, and crocodiles, jellyfish, sharks and stonefish lurking in the water. Even the duckbill platypus has a hook on its hind foot that can deliver a nasty dose and put you in hospital.

I spent a year there after high school working on dairy farms and sheep stations. The most popular tune on the radio in those days was Slim Newton's "Redback on the Toilet Seat," about a spider that bites him. Most of the farms I worked on still had outhouses, and I was warned to take a flashlight with me and give the seat a good bang before I sat down. Fatalities from spider bites even then were fairly rare, but country people were always watchful.

One day, while building a large stack of square bales out in the open, I felt a burning on my ankle and whipped off my boot. A green spider the size of a quarter jumped out and disappeared down a crack between the bales. My boss came over to have a look at the two neat little puncture wounds. He told me to go into the house and let Gramma have a look.

Gramma examined the wound carefully and quizzed me on the colour of the spider. "You sure it was a green one?" she drawled. I said I was quite sure.

"Well," she said after a long pause. "You might get sick. But you wouldn't die." She told me to keep my pants rolled down over my boot tops, because spiders don't like to be "jammed." And she sent me back out to the haystack.

As it turned out, I never did see a redback spider, a funnel-web, a recluse or a wolf. No snakes either. Eventually, my nervousness about poisonous creatures wore off. But one time I was travelling up the coastal highway of Queensland and a farmer invited me to join his crew cutting sugar cane. It was backbreaking work, far more demanding than milking cows or tossing bales of hay. You were always bent over with your face in the canopy, slashing away at the roots of the cane plants with a machete, then slicing the tops off them and throwing big armfuls up on the wagon. I noticed the ground was covered with wisps of black ash, and I asked my employer where it came from.

"That's left over from the burn," he explained. "We set fire to the fields before we come in here. Y'know … to get rid of the tiger snakes."

"Oh," I said and went back to chopping. I chopped for a little while and then I asked, "So, that works, does it? Burning gets rid of the snakes?"

"Yeah, pretty much. We do see the odd one." And then he grinned.

I thought about this for a little bit more and found I couldn't put my face back into the sugar cane canopy and whack away with the same energy as everybody else. At lunchtime I went over to the farmer and told him that maybe the sugar cane business wasn't for me.

"It's the snakes, is it?" said the farmer. "You don't have any snakes at home in Canada?"

I told him about our massasauga rattlesnake that lives in the rocks around Lake Huron and Georgian Bay. It is a pretty timid creature, mildly venomous and seldom bites unless provoked. He raised his eyebrows in astonishment. "Let me get this straight. You have one poisonous snake in Canada … and it rattles?" He told the others and they all roared with laughter.

He patted my shoulder. "No worries, mate. A lot of people tell us they don't like snakes, and I can't blame 'em." He paid me for the morning's work, and I drove on.

I drove up into the Cape York Peninsula, home of the dreaded inland taipan snake and the Australian coral snake, but I never saw one of those either. During the whole trip the only nasty bite I got was from a bull ant that crawled down my boot while I was digging a post pole. It made my foot swell up like a balloon, but again the locals dismissed it, saying it was no more serious than a bee sting.

I did have one brush with a deadly animal on that trip when I climbed up on a retired racehorse and went for a canter in the pasture. I coaxed the old thing into a gentle left-hand turn, not realizing that Australian racehorses only turn to the right. She tilted over like a sailboat in a steady breeze. She kept tilting until she fell right over, with me underneath. I strained my knee and limped for a week, but I survived.

When I got back home, I read that all the poisonous and man-eating animals in Australia together account for only five deaths per year. In the meantime, twenty are killed in horseback riding accidents and another three hundred drown in the ocean. These are pretty much the same statistics the world over. Whether you live in Canada or Mozambique, the rule is the same: always swim between the flags and never, ever get on a horse.

Could be fatal.

ON EXERCISE

꩜

The countryside is traditionally considered the best place to go for a walk. For several weeks of the year in Canada, it often is. But the rest of the time it is too cold or too hot or the wind is howling in your face. Farmers took all the trees down long ago and so there is nothing to stop the wind once it leaves Winnipeg, gathers speed over the Great Lakes and then swoops down from the Niagara Escarpment. It's no fun going for a walk if you have to hold a mitt over your face to breathe.

Still, my doctors are unanimous that I must exercise more. I do manage a form of elliptical weight training every day here at the farm. I climb up and down a ladder and toss bales of hay to the sheep. I wrestle pails of water over gates and clean out pens with a manure fork. There's even a little bit of martial arts involved because I have a Border Cheviot ram named Cato who attacks me whenever my back is turned.

Not so, says my friend Dr. John, a lean, hard-bodied man of science who ran a sports clinic in town for years and made a fortune comforting boomers as their bodies went bad. "That's not exercise. That's just slugging," he said. "You need something aerobic. Why don't you do what I do and get on a bicycle?"

One good reason was the cast John had on his arm from a cycling mishap the week before.

I have always had a bicycle. I pedalled my way around England and France in the summer of 1971, working on farms and picking fruit. It was a lark, but there was always a purpose behind the effort. I was trying to get somewhere cheaply to do something I would be paid for. Even then the roads were clogged with over-oxygenated cyclists with bulging calf muscles and legs shaved to reduce wind resistance. They would fly by in a whoosh of fluorescent Lycra, raising an eyebrow at the kid in jeans and workboots, labouring up the hill to the next pear orchard. If I caught up to them in a pub, their conversation never left the subjects of gear ratios and aerodynamic drag.

Going back to the American Revolution, the Needles family has had no tradition of exercise, and we all live longer than Galapagos tortoises. My dad was the most unathletic person I ever knew and never broke into a trot after the Second World War. He made ninety-seven. He didn't need a hip replacement or knee surgery because all his joints were unused, still in the box. He was an actor for nearly sixty-five years, and people have told me that the most frightening thing they ever saw on stage was my dad in a swordfight. He was legally blind without his glasses. Macbeth and Macduff would flatten themselves against a wall as he went flailing by, usually swinging his sword at the wrong person.

He was also a hypochondriac. He and his mother caught the Spanish flu a few months after he was born in 1919. He never felt quite well again. I wanted to write on his tombstone, "I told you I was sick," but the family opted for an obscure quote from Thomas Gray's *Elegy Written in a Country Churchyard*. Pop believed that good health could be achieved through constant worry and a weekly conversation with his doctors. He outlived them all, and when asked about the secret to longevity he would reply, "I've been vigilant."

"You used to cycle," says my wife, Heath.

"The railroads used to run good hotels," I reply. "Cycling is pretty dangerous. I was knocked off the bike half a dozen times, once by another cyclist and another time by a dog."

The menfolk in Heath's family are cattlemen who fret about prices and the weather, but never about their health. If they can't run something down, they ride it down and rope it. If they can't rope it, they shoot it. I noticed that many of them turned up to our wedding on crutches, which should have been my first clue. My best man predicted darkly that I too would be limping before long, and they were right. I fell out of the haymow about twenty-five years ago and crushed the heel of my left foot. It became arthritic, which deters me from walking, so I went to Dr. John's for cortisone shots until he decided it wasn't the heel after all, but a case of plantar fasciitis. The new treatment is swimming and stretching.

I wasn't opposed to getting back on my old touring bike. Who can argue with a chance to spend less time with the family? I climbed up into the haymow and found it in remarkably good condition, probably because it hadn't been used for forty years. Then it occurred to me, I could bolt the thing into the barn floor and run a chain drive back to the pulley on my oat roller. Instead of risking life and limb out on the road, I could sit here with a cappuccino and a newspaper grinding grain. That way I could feed the cows, feed my body with oxygen and feed my brain with the illusion I was doing something useful.

But the moment passed.

Getting through the
Great Canadian Dark

ϰ

When I bought my farm in 1978, Ontario Hydro wouldn't hook up my house to the grid. They said they had a rule for weekenders. You had to go through a winter first and then decide if you wanted to stay.

If you're going to make it through a winter out here, you'll have to pick up some hobbies like crokinole or tole painting. And it would be a good idea to join a group that will get you out of the house regularly. That's what our community halls and Legions are for.

My own village of Duntroon has smashed up, burned down and worn out three halls since 1833, and we are working on the fourth. Halls always need something—a roof or new siding. In 1997 I gave a talk and raffled off one of my magic chickens at a fundraiser in the village hall. I remember that fundraiser well because it had been snowing hard all day and our road was getting snowed in. So I called Wanda McDermid, the chair of the hall committee, and asked, "Is this thing going ahead tonight?"

And she said, "Oh yes. Why do you ask?"

I said, "Because I'm standing on the veranda and I can't see my car."

"Oh," she said. "It'll settle down before long."

It didn't. It was still snowing hard when Heath and I made our way up the hill in the dark, trying to remember how many hydro poles there are between our sideroad and Duntroon. We were pretty sure we would be the only people there. But when we arrived there were cars parked everywhere and the hall was full. There were even people in wheelchairs. They had hooked up a skipping rope between the parking lot and the front door so that people didn't get lost in the blizzard and wander off up into the escarpment.

Ray Swalm, the tenor for the DufferinAirs barbershop quartet, was delayed by the weather, and the quartet was not prepared to go on without him. He was driving up from Fort Erie. So Wanda said, "It's all right. Danny will just keep talking until Ray gets here."

So I talked and sang and tap-danced until Ray showed up. I remember watching the crowd that evening. They danced all night. They visited and ate and yakked and put on a light lunch at midnight. It was like so many crowds I had seen across rural Canada trooping into Legions and Masonic Halls and arena banquet halls, all absolutely determined to have a good time no matter what was happening anywhere else. I remember thinking how essential this building was to the neighbourhood. How much it reminded me of the Orange Hall in Rosemont where, from the time I was five, I performed on stage in my mother's plays, sang in choirs, learned to dance, had my first swig of rye in a stubby Coke bottle out in the parking lot, got kissed for the first time under the horse chestnut tree in front of the hall, and more.

I remember my mother telling me that the stage had not been built for us. It was put into the new hall when it was built in 1926. And that was the third community hall on the site. Russell Thompson, the Baptist carpenter from Mono Centre, told me that he rode horseback to the opening of the new hall to perform in a play in which he had one of the great one-liners of the evening. He hoisted an axe on his shoulder, opened the kitchen door and announced to the audience, "I'm goin' outside to split some peas for the split-pea soup." That brought the house down, and he was still being called Split Pea Thompson a half century later.

By 1854 Duntroon was having problems with youth vandalism because there was nothing to do all winter and the town had swelled to a population of 1,500. So the village elders formed a Literary and Debating Society. The first debate held in the old meeting house put the following resolution to the floor: "Be it resolved that the cow is superior to the horse." During the debate a fistfight broke out, it turned into a riot, and the hall was wrecked.

The town fathers immediately disbanded the debating society and formed an agricultural society in its place. And they told the young people to put on a fall fair. They tore down the old meeting house and put up a proper Town Hall, made of brick. The first fall fair was held in the summer of 1855 in the pasture just behind that hall.

Then disaster struck. A railway from Toronto bypassed Duntroon 5 miles to the east and everybody moved down the hill to start a new town called Stayner. Duntroon's population dropped to under a hundred and has stayed there ever since.

The people who stayed behind were a determined bunch. When the town of Collingwood took control of the fall fair away from them in a secret meeting and put up a big new headquarters in town, we burned it down. Actually, nobody knows for sure who started the fire, but we were blamed for it. Then Stayner built its own fair building, and we burned that one down too. We kept burning fair buildings until Collingwood finally built one out of brick, steel and asbestos in 1909. A tornado ripped the front off the building in 1910, and they blamed us for that too. But it is still standing. It is called the Curling Club.

In the 1880s one more disaster struck Duntroon. Our new brick Town Hall went up in flames. The Collingwood fire department came out and the chief said it was probably an electrical fault, but we were suspicious about that because we didn't get hydro until 1936. But we built a third hall. It was a modest affair, just a one-storey wooden building without a proper foundation, called the Sons of Scotland. They should have called it the Daughters of Scotland because the women did all the work. But it served the community through two world wars and a depression.

When the floor rotted out of the Sons of Scotland Hall in 1948, we built a fourth one, out of an old military barracks from Camp Borden, which still stands today. It was closed for two years during the pandemic—the first time our village has been deprived of a meeting place since 1833. But on St. Patrick's Day 2022 the hall committee threw open the doors for a Green Beer Day, and a good time was had by all.

In spite of all the changes that have swept over the township, we still have all the small halls that were here thirty-five years ago, and they host countless dances, weddings, anniversaries, euchre parties, coffee clubs, theatrical nights, literary events, political meetings, protests and strawberry suppers, just as they have done since the first settlement here in the early nineteenth century. They are there for you, too.

You Probably Don't
Need a Big House

৵

When I started the addition on my little farmhouse, Hughie heard the backhoe running and came over to observe. "That's a big hole you have there, Danny. It's a beautiful hole. Why don't you fill half of it in?"

There is a repeating pattern in our culture of bright young people who come up with a brilliant new idea, make a fortune in the city and then retire to the country and build a big house.

I once knew a man who immigrated to Canada from Latvia after World War 11 and went to work in a machine shop in southwestern Ontario. He soon saved enough money to buy a small plot and start a market garden. At first he had to borrow most of his equipment, and his neighbour across the road was kind enough to lend him a set of disk ploughs.

But dragging the disks across the road left quite a mark on the highway, and my friend was embarrassed by the damage he had done to a public road. So he rigged up an axle and a hydraulic cylinder and invented what many of his neighbours claim was the first hydraulic-lift disk plough on the continent. The machine shop promptly sold the idea to one of the large farm implement companies and within five years it had spread across North America. My Latvian friend never got a dime and so never got the chance to build a big house.

Max Planck, the famous quantum physicist, once said that the best new ideas never originate from a committee but rather "from the head of an individually inspired researcher who struggles with his problems in lonely thought and unites all his thought on one single point which is his whole world for the moment."

That idea resonates with this lonely researcher, struggling as I do in solitude and without a four-wheel-drive loader tractor. Loading pigs by yourself has a way of uniting your thoughts on a single point. Pigs sense treachery the moment they hear you step off the veranda. When a pig comes up the ramp, sees the guy with the glasses and identifies a weak spot, for an awful moment this becomes your whole world.

Thirty years ago I invented a system for loading pigs that incorporated the principles of the lever, the pulley and the inclined plane. Family and neighbours would gather to witness this wonder of modern agriculture and marvel that it had been created by a mere scribbler. One of the ancients on the sideroad even pronounced it "the slickest way of moving pigs I ever saw." But it never gained traction in the industry.

The farm has been the seedbed for the Western world's technological transformation. Jethro Tull's invention of the seed drill in England in 1701 is widely regarded as the beginning of modern agriculture. Actual farm practices did not change drastically around him until nearly a century later, when pioneers in the New World entered the bottomlands of the Ohio River and tried to turn the heavy clay soils with wooden ploughs. They found that riveting a steel saw blade made in England to the mouldboard would make the plough slide through the clay like butter. Within a short time there were factories next door in New York and Pennsylvania making the first American steel to supply the demand from farmers. In the following years a host of new patents were granted for the chilled steel plough and all the mechanical processes for cultivating, reaping, baling and threshing that we still use today. It is no coincidence that Pittsburgh became the centre of the US steel industry in the process. Technical advances moved so rapidly that by 1880 the Amish and Mennonites called a halt to protect their families and communities from disruption. The rest of us have been trying to catch our breath ever since. In the space of thirty years those farmers yanked agriculture from methods that hadn't changed since biblical times into the modern era.

I am named after an ancestor, Daniel Massey, who laboured in lonely thought in a small forge in Newcastle, Ontario, in the 1840s. He pounded out sturdy farm implements for the community for several decades. His son Hart took over the business, bought several patents from various inventors and went on to build factories in Brantford and later Toronto, where he fabricated ploughs, cultivators, seed drills and finally the reaper-binder that was described as "the world's greatest harvesting machine" at the Exposition Universelle in 1889 in Paris. Queen Victoria used exclusively Massey machinery on her estates. So did Napoleon III. Hart's last act was to build Massey Hall on Shuter Street in Toronto, a place where he could hear the organ music he so loved.

After Hart died in 1896, his third son, my great-grandfather Walter, became president of the company. Walter bought a 400-acre farm 6 miles east of Toronto's Old City Hall, lying between Dawes Road and Victoria Park Avenue. He used it as a laboratory for the company and embarked on a series of firsts. He introduced pasteurized milk to the country, was the first Canadian to take moving pictures and the first to run an electric toy train. He scrapped his carriage for an electric runabout. He named the farm Dentonia Park after his wife, Susan Denton, and raised pigs, chickens and a two-hundred-head herd of Jersey cows. He built a four-storey barn that boasted the first poured concrete floors and large windows across the south side to give the cows more light. Within five years Walter had tripled the size of Massey-Harris and was well on his way to becoming a corporate titan, founding a bicycle company that became CCM and the Toronto City Dairy, which later became Borden's. Unfortunately for the family, Walter drank a glass of bad water on a business trip to Ottawa in 1901 and died of typhoid three weeks later at the age of thirty-seven. He was working on a process for machine-wrapped bread when he died.

The Masseys did not invent anything. They bought the rights to other peoples' inventions. Their real genius lay in their ability to persuade Conservative and Liberal governments to fix tariffs in their favour in both directions: removing them from imported steel and raising them on all farm machinery entering the country. The result was that Canadian farmers paid much higher prices for their machinery than their American counterparts. Walter supported free trade publicly, and the prime minister, Wilfrid Laurier, admired his abilities enough to offer him a Cabinet position. But I have a sneaking suspicion that Walter's fatal excursion to Ottawa probably involved another quiet petition about some pesky tariff.

My mother was raised at Dentonia Park with her three sisters in the only one of the Massey houses that still stands on the old farm. She remembered trotting down the path to watch the cows being milked in the great dairy barn her grandmother still supervised up until 1932, when the American dairy conglomerate Borden's bought the City Dairy. Mother loved the smell of those gentle Jersey cows, and when she bought her own farm in 1955 she started her own herd, finding pedigrees that she thought might have originated at Dentonia.

I have often wondered what to make of my family legacy. It's pretty clear the wheels came off the bus after my great-grandfather's death. Without his creative energy, the City Dairy and his bicycle company ran into difficulty almost immediately. His widow took his seat on the board of Massey-Harris, but she soon gave up the house on Shuter Street and moved her young family permanently to the Dentonia Park farm. The Masseys were new money in Toronto and never felt completely comfortable or accepted among the FOOFs, the fine old Ontario families like the Jarvises and Boultons. That helps to explain the extraordinary amount of philanthropic building the family did. At Dentonia, Susan dressed in black to mourn her husband and reigned in feudal splendour for the next thirty years. Her brother-in-law Chester Massey, a deeply religious invalid, moved his home there from Jarvis Street, bringing his boys, Raymond and Vincent. When Susan's three daughters married, they each built spacious homes on the farm, on 5-acre lots. They built a 12-foot-high board fence all the way down Dawes Road to shield them from the sight and sounds of a city rapidly rolling toward them. And they settled down to life on the farm as Toronto's first urban refugees. But what a strange farm it was! It had a cricket pitch and tennis courts. Ring-necked pheasants roamed the grounds, and waterfowl swam in many ponds. The pastures began to grow up into a massive oak, maple and elm forest.

Of all the memoirs written and stories I have heard about that magical place and time, no one ever mentions doing any farm work. Nobody picked up a pitchfork and went to the fields to gather hay to winter the cows. That was work for other people, who were referred to by their last names. Instead, the family got very interested in two subjects: public health, because it was bad water that had felled the last, best hope of the family, and high culture, because it represented a break from the pinched, teetotalling Methodist teachings of their forebears and a way to leave their mark on a plodding, bumptious city known as Hogtown.

Susan struck up an acquaintance with Charles "Trick" Currelly, the charismatic archaeologist who was then roaming the world looting treasures from failed states. Susan offered him the hoard of Egyptian artifacts her husband had shipped home from his world travels and helped Currelly fund the construction of the Royal Ontario Museum. Her sister-in-law Lillian Massey founded the Domestic Science program at University of Toronto and built another stone pile across the street from the new museum, where she and Adelaide Hoodless, the founder of the Women's Institute, carried a new creed of food safety to the hinterlands. Chester built Burwash Hall for Victoria College at the University of Toronto. His son Vincent served as Dean of Men and tried to take on responsibility for the family business, although he was more interested in the theatre than he was in making ploughs and binders. And they all put on theatricals in the open air on the lawns of Dentonia Park when weather permitted.

Susan eventually started work on an enormous one-hundred-room mansion with a theatre seating two hundred, an indoor heated swimming pool, an assembly hall, a library, common rooms, a hospital, a billiard room, a dark room for photography, showers, a small gymnasium, a museum and other rooms that were never occupied while she owned it. She kept fourteen servants in the house plus gardeners and other staff to run the dairy barn and the farm.

Not surprisingly, the enriched atmosphere of Dentonia Park launched a remarkable cadre of young people, sending the boys to higher education at Oxford, Harvard, MIT and McGill. The two most famous products were Chester's sons. Raymond left in the 1920s to make a career as an actor on the West End stage in London and later in Hollywood films. Vincent attended Oxford, where he became stuffier than the stuffiest British aristocrat and returned home determined to build Jerusalem in his hometown, the outpost of an empire he very much admired. At Oxford he met my grandfather Arthur Goulding, decided he was clever and brought him back to Dentonia, where Arthur fell in love with Susan's daughter Dorothy and married her, joining the growing troupe on the estate. With Massey Foundation money, Vincent envisioned Hart House as a boy's club (and a place where he could escape the formidable presence of his Aunt Susan). If you think I'm making that up, have a look at the inscription chipped into stone on the way into the Great Hall. Edited for brevity, it basically says, "No Girlz." Vincent lacked the common touch and was defeated in his one attempt at getting elected to the House of Commons. Lord Salisbury, a member of the aristocratic Cecil family, which dates to the Crusades in England, worked with him for several years at Whitehall in London as Dominion Secretary and his boss. Salisbury famously said, "Young Vincent is a fine chap but does make one feel like a bit of a savage."

Vincent's way of compensating for the family's parvenu status in Toronto was to cultivate an air of effortless superiority. He loved dress-up, and his uniforms in later life made him look like a comic opera figure. Vincent badgered his aunt into selling the family company and then switched to the diplomatic service, where he rose quickly through the ranks. Prime Minister Mackenzie King couldn't stand him and took every opportunity to post him outside the country, first as Canada's representative at the League of Nations and later as high commissioner to Government House in London through the war. With effortless superiority Vincent supported appeasement of Hitler until the winds finally changed and war became inevitable. Then he smoothly adjusted his sails to support the war effort. He never met a lord he didn't like. He pestered prime ministers repeatedly for a knighthood long after the government had decided imperial titles were no longer appropriate for Canadians. Louis St. Laurent appointed him the first Canadian-born governor general in 1952, and he was miffed that George VI died suddenly and messed up the pomp and pageantry that was supposed to be accorded the swearing-in of a new GG. At Rideau Hall he formed the Canada Council for the Arts and lobbied for a Canadian set of decorations, the Order of Canada, which was finally instituted in 1967, the year he died.

Meanwhile back at the ranch, when the Depression struck in 1929 Susan was appalled at the terrifying cost of maintaining what she cheerfully called "Susan's Folly." Two years later she did the sensible thing and gave it all away. The great house plus 25 acres of the farm went to Crescent School for Boys. She sold the dairy herd and donated the rest of the farm to the township of East York for a park. Then she moved into the Selby Hotel on Sherbourne Street, the same hotel where legend has it Ernest Hemingway wrote *Farewell to Arms*. She died there in 1943. Her family at Dentonia floated along, living on the fumes of her fortune for another thirty years until everyone drifted away or died, and then … it was all gone.

In the years after she left Dentonia, amateur theatre took hold of the remaining group. My grandmother Dorothy founded the Toronto Children's Players, an amateur troupe that performed in the Eaton Auditorium on the seventh floor of Eaton's College Street building from 1931 to 1959. At times during the Depression it was the only live theatre in Toronto. Grandfather the doctor gave up his medical practice and tacked together stage sets with the chauffeur, Bill Cook. I remember Grandfather as a lofty and remote figure who wandered around the estate with a shotgun blasting at blackbirds. If he spoke to us at all it was in rhyming Edwardian couplets, encouraging us to be seen and not heard. My mother began writing plays for the troupe when she was eight, and she and her sisters began speaking as if they were on stage in front of a large audience. The girls were encouraged above everything else to "be interesting," which meant they got into the habit of saying anything they liked, and they fought like alley cats for half a century. I called them the Four Sisters of the Apocalypse: Hysteria, Hypothermia, Hypochondria and Hypoglycemia—and for some reason they never took offence. When my grandmother died the sisters approached me and asked if I would do a reading for the funeral at Grace Church on-the-Hill, some poem about Egypt. When I finished the reading and looked up, all four of them were weeping freely in the front row. I was puzzled by this, but my Aunt Susan explained afterward that it was as if Dr. Goulding had come back to life and was reading for his wife's funeral. This made me feel terribly uncomfortable.

"I didn't like him," I blurted. "I always thought he was a pompous, ponderous know-it-all!"

"Yes," Susan smiled. "You are so much like him."

That made me reflect. Perhaps I had missed something about the old boy. There must have been more to him than I thought.

The trust fund that my great-grandfather Walter left in 1901 was finally disbursed the year after that funeral. The family accountant presented each of us with a cheque for $12,000 and sadly informed us that we would now have to work for a living. I managed to hang onto that bequest for five years and then used it as a down payment for my own farm. The last cow from my mother's herd, Haystack's Roxanne, arrived in 1990 and I milked her by hand until she died three years later. I really should have spread her ashes with her ancestors at Dentonia, but she went off on the dead stock wagon as was the rural custom at the time.

The only other inheritance I received from Dentonia Park was my friend Rod Beattie, who strangely enough was born in Chester Massey's old house on the farm in 1948, when the building was being used to house teaching staff for Crescent School. Rod's family moved a block away from us in North Toronto in the 1950s, and our younger brothers went to a theatre school run by Jack Medhurst, another of my grandmother Dorothy's protegés from Toronto Children's Players. Rod and I did theatre together at Hart House through university, and we eventually formed a partnership for the Wingfield Farm plays, which is still in place forty years later.

The point of all this is that I drive along the escarpment today and see dozens of massive houses, second and third homes, most of which stand empty for months on end. Some of them rival Great-Grandmama's pile. I was reading about an archaeological dig in Tibet where researchers have uncovered the remains of Kublai Khan's "stately pleasure dome," the palace he built out in the countryside for when he needed to get away from the capital. He used it as a headquarters while he ruled a third of the world's population in the thirteenth century. The workers measured the foundations, and I was surprised to learn that the building was about 500 square feet smaller than the house a dentist built just up the road from us.

So the lesson here is that you should not build a big house when you come out to the country. It will collect mountains of useless stuff and you'll inevitably get sick of it and give it all away in the end, as Great-Grandmama did. But by all means build a shop out the back because if you're lucky, one of your children will struggle in lonely thought out there and come up with a really good idea, something that will help him get back to the city to make a good living when he grows up.

Where Good Ideas
Come From

&

Writing and farming may not appear to have much in common, but writing is linked to every human activity. Consider these titles in a single row on my bookshelf:

How to Cure the Problem Horse
Making Twig Furniture
Goat Husbandry
Easy Pruning
The Home Smoker
General Principles of Small Engine Repair
Weeds of Ontario
Raising Sheep the Modern Way
The International Poultryman's Handbook
Important Poultry Diseases
Matching the Hatch (Fly-Tying)

I'm embarrassed to say these volumes are all well thumbed. They flow from the imaginations of people who have filled themselves up with so much information on a subject that they leak wisdom and feel a burning need to share it with others to encourage human progress.

I have been pounding a keyboard for fifty years now, and I don't type one whit faster on this computer than I did on an Underwood typewriter in 1974. There has been no giant tech leap forward for me. This business of shaping a sentence in the English language resists mechanizing the way certain crops like lion's mane mushrooms and ginseng refuse to be mass-produced. It takes a shepherd.

People forget that it was the lonely writer who forged the gap between hardware and software in the computer industry. Computers could do a lot of things, but they were at a dead loss when it came to handling the subtleties of the English language. The blinking lights and whirring tapes needed a special "soft" program to supervise the works, and that program in turn needed guidance from a human operator. The machine needed husbandry, the vigilance of the poul-tryman and the attentiveness of the gardener.

This may help to explain why the countryside has produced so many aftermarket genius inventors, about one every 5 square miles by my brother-in-law's estimate. Terry Sheridan, who runs a machine shop in town, built a miniature bulldozer for his five-year-old son. It weighed about 800 pounds, and the lad could take his sandbox pretty much anywhere he liked. Terry has also revived the lost art of making corn brooms.

The market for children's bulldozers and authentic corn brooms has been slow to develop, but this doesn't stop him.

"My brain is a public resource," he insists. "Like a library or a light-house. Just to know that people have made use of my idea to better their lives is the only compensation I need."

My editor for many years at *Country Guide*, Peter Gredig, pioneered Manifold Cuisine, a variety of recipes that could be whipped up on the manifold of a John Deere 4400 combine. His cookbook is sadly out of print. The combine coffee perk was an early effort that showed promise. Field Pizza Pops take about three minutes to make … a little less if the machine has turbo, and a lot less if it needs a water pump. His TV dinners were interesting, but I could never eat the peas. For the last ten years Peter has been working on the combine toaster. He figures that the first company that turns out a combine that can do toast will sweep the market.

One reason our inventors don't pursue patents vigorously could be the liability factor. Wilf Smalley invented the motion-activated barn gate opener, which attempted to mimic the success of the garage door opener so popular in the suburbs. However, Wilf's gate was set off by anything from a passing taxi to a cell phone, and when it malfunctioned the results were frequently memorable.

ON THE RURAL SCHOOL

෴

My mother used to say, "The British have had public education for two hundred years and it has had no noticeable effect on the population."

She taught school from the age of sixteen, a trick her father, the eye doctor, organized by taking his wife and four daughters on extended tours of prewar Europe and on their return announcing to the authorities in Toronto that all of his daughters had completed their education. No one protested or asked for evidence. By 1939 teachers were in short supply, and you could qualify for the profession by doing a six-week course and writing a test. It probably helped that my mother's grandmother had donated her big house to Crescent School for Boys just a few years earlier, and the gift must have been fresh on the principal's mind when Mrs. Massey's granddaughter appeared at the door looking for work. Mother soon found herself teaching unruly boys of roughly her own age, which must have been a life-altering experience for her. She always said that dealing with adolescents was like being a submarine commander. "If you can't drink tea without your hand shaking, don't drink tea."

Just a few weeks before Queen Elizabeth died, my family gathered in a small country cemetery in Mono Township north of Toronto to bury Mother's ashes, a ceremony postponed for two years by the pandemic. The cemetery was just a few miles from the 100-acre pasture farm she bought in 1955 to use as a writer's retreat. The farm had just been sold after serving for more than sixty years as a centre for the family.

At the interment ceremony we walked past a row of gravestones marked with the names of neighbours, friends and more than a few of Mother's archrivals. For she had a sharp tongue. She lost her job as the host of *Kindergarten of the Air* on CBC Radio partly because she famously snapped at an executive meeting, "The directors of the fall fair do a better job of managing things and they've all been drunk for two weeks before the fair!" When she put silver candlesticks on the altar of St. Luke's, a woman wrote to the bishop denouncing her as a "papist."

She was indifferent to criticism. She dove into the Rosemont community with great energy and carved out a role for herself as the church organist and choir leader, a Women's Institute member and the director of a theatre troupe of farm kids who performed plays she wrote and directed. The first plays were performed in front of the neighbours on the lawn of our farmhouse in late August after several weeks of drama classes and rehearsals. Neighbours came down to the farm with picnic hampers and folding chairs and lined up their cars with the headlights on to provide stage lighting. After three seasons we moved up to the Orange Hall in Rosemont, where the weather was more predictable.

She battled with nearly every minister at the church over the next thirty years and was finally banned from the hall permanently when she removed King William's portrait and nailed a crucifix in its place for a production of *Maria Chapdelaine*. It wasn't until the last Orangeman died three years later and the Lodge was decommissioned that she was allowed to resume her culture series for the community.

When I was nine and writing my first speech for a competition at school, she suggested I write about the Seventh Line. "This is a world that is slipping away," she said. "You should pay attention to it." At the time she was working on a novel called *Margaret*, about an Irish workhouse girl who finds her way to a hill farm in Mono Township in the 1840s. It was finally published in 1966.

We all attended S.S. no. 17, the two-room school in Rosemont, a Gothic red-brick building that still stands on the highway west of the village. Mother would move us out to the farm in early May and return us to the city at the end of October, which meant changing schools twice a year. Some school superintendent made the mistake of telling her she couldn't do that, and so she did that for the next decade.

"I told the silly fathead that children need to learn to adapt above anything else. Of course, being a superintendent, he had no idea what I was talking about." There was no bus for primary school students in those days until my mother bought a used St. John Ambulance van with a raised roof for moving wheelchair patients, painted it green and picked up all the kids on the Seventh Line every morning as she delivered us, including a boy on crutches from polio. At the end of the season, after the Hallowe'en party at the school, we packed up and moved back to the city to attend a winter session at Allenby Public School in North Toronto. The kids from the Rosemont neighbourhood still recall the sight of Mother's green van navigating the potholes down the Seventh Line as a more reliable sign of spring than any robin.

The quality of education was not high in either place, but it didn't matter much to Mother because she had taught us all to read and write well before we went near the building. "Literacy is too important to be left to a school," she said. Mrs. Raeburn, an elderly woman with Coke-bottle glasses and a concrete white hairdo, supervised us through the upper four grades at S.S. no. 17. I remember her circulating a paragraph for us to parse that ran: "The British Empire is made up of all kinds of people who get along real peaceable." The morning routine started with the national anthem, "God Save the Queen," and the Lord's Prayer. Then we were each required to answer the Three Questions: Have you brushed your teeth, combed your hair and drunk a glass of water? Then it was time for the morning news on CFRB radio with Jack Dennett, who occupied a place in Mrs. Raeburn's holy trinity along with her dead husband and John Diefenbaker. After the news we began lessons. Recess and lunch hour was one-up baseball. The school had no running water, just a hand pump outside above a cistern. The building had an interesting mix of smells: disinfectant from the lavatories, egg salad sandwiches and horse poop from Jasper Brett's pony tied up beside the woodshed. I much preferred the smells of no. 17 to the entirely industrial smells of Allenby: more disinfectant, alcohol from the Gestetner duplicating machines, hot asphalt and the human aroma of six hundred overheated bodies in the same building.

For most of my time at S.S. no. 17 I coached other children with their reading. In the afternoon we were encouraged to read from any one of the books in a tall cupboard at the back of the class that served as the school library. By this time I was reading a book a day, and Mrs. Raeburn decided I was showing off. So she instituted a rule that you were limited to one book a week. The loophole was that you could spend any amount of time at the back, choosing that book. So I read a lot of books standing up and made a point of taking only the fattest and heaviest one back to my desk.

Thirty-five years later my wife and I taught our own children to read before they started school in the village of Duntroon. There were fewer than a hundred students at the time, and the school was already on the hit list to be closed. The parents ran a rearguard action to keep it open for the next nineteen years but ultimately admitted defeat.

I discovered there had been no great leap forward in education between S.S. no. 17 of 1960 and Duntroon Public of 2000. Mrs. Raeburn's loony fondness for Jack Dennett and John Diefenbaker had been replaced by a general zeal for recycling and endangered species. Most of my children's classmates would have been classified as candidates for remedial English by S.S. no. 17 standards and placed in my care. The children ignored the long list of contradictory commandments pasted on the wall of the main hallway, entreating them to show kindness but keep hands off, work hard but not compete too vigorously for scarce resources. By the age of ten every child understood that none of these rules had any traction outside the bubble-wrapped world of the school. They also knew that you couldn't fail anybody for anything.

When I complained about this to my mother, she waved me away with her ivory cigarette holder. "Education was never very effective, dear. But at least it could be fun. The real problem is it isn't much fun anymore." Her big mouth had narrowed her options in the big city once again. The program she ran for the Etobicoke Board of Education promoting Drama in Education and Three-Dimensional Learning had been curtailed and finally chopped entirely by the early 1980s. She returned to Rosemont to run an antique shop, which was an odd fit because she was not that fond of the public, and referred to her customers as the Look Mabels. I often thought I should put up a sign on the veranda of the shop for the benefit of those leaving: "You're not special. She talks like that to everybody."

The word "education" comes from the Latin *educare*, meaning "to lead out." Darkness is what we assume we are leading the little darlings out of, except we aren't really doing much of that anymore. We are mostly leading them from darkness into a thick fog. Stupidity management has prevailed in school boards and ministries for so long that Mother was right. It isn't much fun anymore. One of the last holdouts for fun was Duntroon Central School. In that school in that decade there was still a balance between eyes and acres. Despite the faceless bureaucracy that drove everything else in the county, DCS conformed to the ancient rules of the village because of its size: a place where everyone knew your name and at least a slice of your story. You weren't required to like all of these people, but at least you knew each other, and you had a vague understanding that this might come in handy someday for something.

Peggy White laboured heroically with each of the children to teach them math, but her true value came to light when she coached the boys' basketball team. With fewer than a hundred students, DCS had a shallow gene pool to draw from for basketball or any other competitive sport. At every inter-school tournament, the supervisors routinely shut off the score clock once Duntroon was down 50–0 to prevent feelings from being hurt too badly. But somehow the Duntroon team never lost its fighting spirit. They always came off the court flushed and in high spirits, complimenting each other on a closely fought game. Miss White explained to me that this was because the kids had developed their own scoring system unrelated to whatever numbers showed on the clock. Big Shane, who was the tallest kid in the school but slow moving, would walk down to the opposing team's net and stand under it waiting for someone to heave the ball in his direction. Every so often he would get hold of it, but he was a terrible shot. So the other boys decided that if Shane just hit the rim of the hoop, then it was worth two points. That explained why they all high-fived each other whenever Shane appeared to miss a shot. It also explains why the basketball team has stayed friends ever since.

One of the principals during that time, John Campbell, was a great educator. He walked around the hallways with a bemused smile on his face as if he found the whole business delightfully entertaining.

"Dan," he confided to me once. "I'm worried about your marks.

This is the fourth reptile project you've handed in and you've got a frog on it. Surely you know by now that a frog is an amphibian."

I asked him if he had ever seen a science project completed by a student without assistance from a parent. "No," he replied. "But I've only been doing this for thirty-five years, so there's still time."

My younger son struggled with reading until John called us in and made a suggestion. He had observed that Matthew loved making models and he suggested that we make space at home where Matt could work on his models undisturbed. "He'll teach himself to read doing the models," said John. We did as John suggested, and Matt not only taught himself to read but became a gifted illustrator and now does freelance work for a national magazine.

At roughly the time my youngest daughter cleared the building and I was battling with two teenagers, I remember making a visit to my mother at her home in Rosemont. She poured me two fingers of Scotch and told me to sit.

"Every time you come down here you bitch about your children," she said. "Why don't you just ignore them? That's what I did with you, and you turned out fine. You need a hobby. I notice you like chickens. Get yourself more chickens."

Mother was terrific at free-ranging children. She operated in the years before parenting became a verb. She and my father made a vow at the altar that children were never going to interfere with their lives. They believed that children needed vast amounts of unsupervised time if they were to grow and develop properly. We were given that time because my father was never home, always on a bus somewhere to play a part in a theatre troupe in some remote corner of the country. And my mother had her own career as a teacher, radio personality, author, playwright, director, filmmaker, patron of the arts, public speaker and intrepid traveller. Mother was always busy doing something far more interesting than parenting. Almost as soon as we arrived in Mono Township she began farming us out to the families on the Seventh Line, often for weeks at a time. If we complained about the disruption to our lives she would say, "The dinosaurs died out because they couldn't learn to adapt. The lower the animal, the harder to adjust. Are you a low form of life?" Later in life I learned that there was no scientific evidence to support her notion that species are organized in a hierarchy. The dinosaurs lived 350 times longer than we have, so they must have had something going for them. And they died out because a meteor hit the earth, not because they couldn't change their habits when the world changed. But I didn't know enough to put forward any of those arguments at the time, and so I was sent to live at the Bretts' farm at the very top of the Seventh Line, the second-highest point in southern Ontario.

Dorothy Brett was the other teacher at S.S. no. 17. She taught the lower grades and lived on a real farm with beef cows, workhorses, sheep, pigs and a large henhouse. Her husband, Keith, owned three farms, thanks to the hard-headed business sense of his father, Earl, who was still around when I started visiting with them. Earl was a humourless man who carried a cattle cane and rapped any animal he met smartly on the snout with it. I disliked him thoroughly and didn't understand why Dorothy always placed me beside him at the dinner table. Apparently I was the only one who talked more than he did and could compete with him in conversation. This gave the rest of the table some relief, and the family always welcomed me when Mother dropped me off.

My teacher was also my neighbour, and my hostess, and my mother's close friend, and more of a hands-on grandmother to me than either of my biological ones. It appalled me when kids disobeyed Dorothy or spoke disrespectfully to her.

My kids had similar relationships with their teachers at DCS, some of whom had decided their way to this small rural school with a village atmosphere. But the county school board had a fixed notion of the minimum number of students to justify a public school, and DCS did not meet that number. When they encountered fierce resistance to their efforts to close it, the board opted for a reliable bureaucratic method for wearing down opposition: they nitpicked it to death. It took a few more years, but the building closed without a whimper in 2012. In the meantime the decline of the rural school continues. In our town, in spite of a period of rapid growth, every hundred new houses built produces only five children for the school system.

Leaving aside the deterioration of standards and the mind-numbing bureaucracy, going to school still leaves the opportunity for free-ranging a child if you have a few acres. I never had my mother's nerve when it came to letting my own children discover their world unsupervised, but they did it anyway. They often tell war stories of all the adventures and trouble they got into while I was busy typing and their mother was baking made-to-order cakes. I think their experience of the rural setting was what a modern educator would call "enriched."

Just recently I was finally banned by the Peel District School Board, which is an honour bestowed on a select few of my favourite writers: Mark Twain for *Huckleberry Finn*, W.P. Kinsella for *The Fencepost Chronicles*, Margaret Atwood for *The Handmaid's Tale*. I'm afraid my sin was fairly minor, like a parking infraction where others were planning an assault on the Capitol. My sin was writing a musical with Christmas in the title. It doesn't take much to get into trouble these days. The ancient prophet sure nailed it when he wrote in Proverbs 28:1, "The wicked run when no one is chasing them."

In Praise of
the Farm Dog

~

You'll want a dog, if for no other reason than to tie you to the place and make you return home at nights. Not just any dog, either. You'll want a farm dog, which is more of a type than a breed, a type often referred to as a borderline collie.

My vet doesn't do dogs. He knows all about dogs after seven years at the vet college and a brief stint interning at an urban clinic, but when he opened a practice specializing in large animals, he made it known he was leaving the dog and cat business to others.

So when my farm dog got hit on the road and was limping, I was surprised that Jason offered to take a look at him. I asked why he would make an exception in my case, and he said:

"Because he's a farm dog. And you're not an idiot."

I took that as a great compliment. Over time I learned that Jason didn't mind doing anything for farmers because they have a completely different mindset than almost all other people who own animals.

"When animals have a clear commercial purpose and are not your pets, it's easier to form an emotional cocoon and make practical decisions," he said. He called this way of looking at the world "farmer thinking," and we still trade examples of it whenever we visit.

"When you go out to a farm, you'll find the farmer standing beside the feeder looking at a dead cattle beast lying on the ground," he said. "And the first words out of that man's mouth will be, 'What have I done wrong here, doctor?' Of course, he hasn't done anything wrong at all. But you get so you look forward to helping that guy out and making his day a little better."

When I was a kid in Mono Township, we had a dog catcher named Ernie Dods who believed that farm dogs should be tax exempt. He had three questions that established eligibility: "Did you pay for that dog? Does the dog go in the house? Has he ever been to town?" If you answered no to all three questions, he would bid you "G'day" and drive on.

Those were the days. The dog tax in Clearview Township is now $30 a snout, and the program brings in more revenue than the development tax on new houses.

The farm dog of yesteryear was a fat, cheerful collie with fleas and a way of curling his lip in a toothy grin that made visitors get back in the car. When you drove up the lane he would say *woof!* about four times and flop back down in the flowerbed that Mother had pretty much given up on since he was a pup. If you patted him you were careful just to pat the top of his head, because if you touched him anywhere else your hand would smell bad. He brought the cows in if he was in the mood. The rest of the time he sat by the house chewing on a dead groundhog and snapping at flies. He lived on table scraps and sour milk and slept in the woodshed. On the coldest days of the year he might be allowed in the summer kitchen, but he was never, ever allowed to cross the threshold into the main house. He was never taken into town, and he wasn't interested anyway. All he needed was within eyesight of the veranda. He got nothing for his health apart from a rabies shot every spring, administered by his owner, and usually lived to the age of fourteen without once receiving the undivided attention of a vet. Then one day his back legs would seize up and he'd stop eating and his owner would take him for a slow walk back to the bush, a walk from which only one would return. A noticeable silence would hang over the farmstead for a few weeks and then a new puppy would appear on the veranda.

The first dog that came to this farm was a little Jack Russell terrorist my wife brought with her when we were married. Andy was born in the drawer of a bedroom dresser, one of five puppies that roamed her parents' farm like a motorcycle gang, fought ruthlessly under the dinner table and sang "Edelweiss" on the couch whenever Father picked up his accordion. He had a vocabulary of over a hundred words, mostly profanity he had picked up from me. I dragged him out of countless scrapes with other dogs, and he had more scratches and dents on him than a farm truck. He was wonderful with babies and small children. He was terrible with chickens. He was also a plain damn nuisance.

Now that I think of it, you might want to get a shorter-haired dog than a collie, just to make it easier to get the burrs out of him. Andy never picked up a burr, but you really don't want any kind of terrier because they pick fights with skunks, raccoons and, worst of all, porcupines. So maybe a mutt collie is best, after all. I have trouble making up my mind. Absolutely no beagles, because they are heartbreaking wanderers. No miniatures (because they are coyote food) and no watchdogs (they get you into trouble eventually).

There's no reason to listen to me. I have a long-legged livestock protection dog who hails from Turkey. Well, he's not purebred. He's probably one-part Akbash and about three parts Walmart Greeter. We got him when my wife's mother could no longer care for herself at the farm, and she and the dog both came to live with us until she died.

Like most livestock dogs, Dexter had lived outside in all weather for five years at that point. He was very reluctant to cross the threshold, and I had to explain to him that if he wanted to spend time with his mother, he would have to come in.

He shrugged and padded into the kitchen. After a pause he said, "You have central air." That was the beginning. He slept on the floor beside Gramma until she died and then he moved into the master bedroom, which has a bay window and a commanding view of the sheep pasture. He assured me he could keep track of the sheep just fine from the bed and he would certainly let me know if there were any problems. We invested in a king-size bed to ensure there was enough room for us too.

As it turned out, he didn't do sheep. Sheep didn't make sense to him, and he ignored them. He roams the farm every morning and does the rounds of the farms next door peeing on fenceposts and woofing authoritatively from time to time to let coyotes know he's on duty. The rest of the time he lies in the middle of the Blind Line greeting any car that comes down our way. For a long time he didn't like birds flying overhead, but once I explained chickens to him he decided everything with feathers got a free pass. His head is about window height, and he has that crinkly-nose grin that makes people wonder if it's wise to open the car door. He's actually saying, "Mum just made biscuits. Do you want to come in?"

We've had Dexter for seven years now, and we've worn the fur off the top of his head patting him. His ears are so soft he could do an endorsement for Delsey bathroom tissue.

When the pandemic started, my wife gathered us all together at the dinner table and told us very firmly that the most important thing we could do was look after each other as best we can. Dexter was listening attentively, and the next day he went out on his morning patrol and brought back a turkey. I don't mean a mouldy wild turkey carcass from the woods. This was a shrink-wrapped 10-pound Grade A Cavalier bird from Walmart. I called around the neighbours to see where he might have found it, and old John McKee said, "Danny, that's a good dog. I think he is possibly a breeder. Did he eat much of it?"

I said, "Just one of the legs."

"That's fair," said John. "It's about 15 percent, which is a reasonable finder's fee. He's doing curbside pickup for you."

There's a fine line between curbside pickup and porch pirate. Dexter has a milk-and-cookies route he follows every day around the Ninth Concession, no matter the weather, and it takes him to every corner of this farm and the ones next door too. He wants us to believe that he keeps us safe from coyotes, but this is a harmless fiction. The truth is he craves news and gossip as much as any of us, and he makes more of an effort to find both. He seldom comes when called, although he does stop when he hears my voice, even if he is 500 yards away. He waves his tail enthusiastically, woofs and carries on his way. When he does finally come home, he sits on the hill across from the house in the sheep pasture and sings for about ten minutes—or, as my wife says, he "hoos." It is a joyous sound, and it gave us special comfort during the isolation.

In this household we often ask, "Why can't you be more like Dexter?" Why can't you just drop the bag of hammers and find something to be delighted about? Why can't we rise with the sun, trot out to the sheep pasture, sit down and sing a hymn of praise and thanks for the beauty and the endless distractions of this corner of the earth?

I had some difficulty following my own advice during the lockdowns, with every theatre closed and no engagements for what seemed like the rest of my life. I read about people in downtown condos taking advantage of the solitude by learning jazz piano or finally figuring out how to podcast, and it all sounded very creative and therapeutic. But thankfully the farm is a jealous mistress and would not be ignored.

The farm cares nothing for pandemics and stock market meltdowns when a new growing season is about to begin with all its rigid deadlines and moving parts. It requires constant vigilance.

That summer I went on to raise my chickens, lambs and pigs, found hay and straw, coaxed bushel baskets of vegetables and fruit out of the garden and orchard. The well survived the dry weather. While a freighter went sideways in the Suez Canal and store shelves emptied out, nothing distracted us from stocking the freezers and cupboards with another season's produce and piling three bush cords of firewood against the side of the house. For once, the farm seemed like a well-ordered place compared to the rest of the world. This should come as no surprise. Small enterprises have always been the most reliable and resilient vehicles to travel in when the world hits a series of speed bumps.

It was not, however, a good time to consult the health care system about anything serious, so when Heath suffered another heart attack last year, we had a number of sleepless nights. But then the specialists announced that she had a special condition called a spontaneous coronary arterial dissection, which usually only happens to women and, like a lot of things that happen to women, they fix it themselves.

After a few months on blood thinners, my wife has been restored to her garden and kitchen, a reminder that science and the modern world has given us a lot to be grateful for, not the least of which is hearing your name called a lot during the day.

On Animal Rights, Sustainable Farming and Other Delicate Subjects

~

There's an old joke that you should always have the ingredients for making a martini when you go into the woods or the desert. That way if you become hopelessly lost and are in despair of ever being found, you can start mixing a martini and someone will pop over your shoulder and tell you that you are doing it wrong. Then you are saved. The know-it-alls of today have moved away from martinis and decided to be experts on all matters relating to food. Everything now must be organic, natural, fair trade, chemical and cage-free, picked by single mothers within a hundred miles of you, carbon neutral and, of course, completely sustainable.

I was in a little arts and craft shop last week when I heard an earnest young woman with two children in tow grilling the saleswoman about a basket of "densely felted organic dryer balls" sitting in a basket beside the till.

"Are they made of natural fibres?" asked the young woman.

"Yes," said the saleswoman. "They are made entirely of wool. Organic and completely natural."

"Oh," said the customer. "I believe in animal rights. After the wool is taken, does the sheep have a good life?"

That stumped the saleswoman. She was not a sheep person, and she couldn't really say. I am a sheep person, and I had plenty to say about the life of a sheep. But to my credit, I remained silent. What I wanted to say is that for the last 6,000 years, ever since the ancient Sumerians started peeling the wool off sheep and spinning the fibres, we have been growing wool on their backs. If you don't shear a sheep regularly, it will sicken and die. To answer the woman's question directly, yes, the sheep definitely has a better life sheared than left in its natural state.

Sheep have been looked after for so long that they can't survive very long without the attention of a shepherd. This was already true 2,500 years ago and is one of the reasons sheep appear so often in the Bible. Like people, they need a lot of supervising. Left to their own devices they always get into trouble. Dogs run them to death, wolves sneak in and kill them one at a time, they eat wild cherry leaves and keel over. They roll into holes and can't get up. They walk over cliffs. If they break through a hole in the fence, they walk into the nearest farm outbuilding and you can just hear them asking, "What's toxic in here, Marj?"

Animals do not have rights. If they did, they would also have responsibilities, and that would make a cat a murderer, which is absurd. I am the one with the rights, not the sheep. With my rights come a set of strict responsibilities, the chief one being an obligation to practise stewardship of all things in my care. Stewardship is a stern and demanding calling, and few people understand this more clearly than a shepherd, who practises one of the oldest professions on the planet.

It's surprising I have anything to do with sheep. Two hundred years ago my ancestors were tossed off the land during the clearances in Scotland and replaced by sheep. My forefathers (and the mothers too) were shipped across the Atlantic in leaky ships and forced to make a new life in places even a sheep would have found unforgiving. No one ever talked about a sheep's rights in those days. That's because they were too busy trying to figure out how to protect their own rights without ending up swinging by a rope in a public square.

Today, we have time to reflect on any theological question we choose to explore. And we are so well fed that we now have the energy to bully anyone who doesn't agree with us, even if our beliefs are constructed like a cucumber frame. After thirty years with sheep, I know that I am obliged to protect them from predators and parasites, bad weather and the poor life choices for which they are famous. In return I take the wool, which they do not need. Some of them will go into the freezer, but again, all my efforts are designed to ensure that those sheep only know one bad day.

Wind turbine politics grinds away in our neighbourhood just as they have for more than a decade. The two sides stopped listening to each other a long time ago. Some would take this as evidence that we live in a polarized society. I think it's because neither side has ever had its day in court. People need to be heard before they settle for a group decision. The *Green Energy Act* of 2009 decreed that exceptions would not be tolerated in the headlong pursuit of wind and solar energy. That was a serious mistake, and the legislation was repealed ten years later. The Pope himself has said that a politician's job is to lead the conversation, not force ideology down the public throat.

I once got dragged into the middle of a heated discussion about wind energy while working as a volunteer at the Collingwood fair. We had tried to inject some life into the sheep show by offering a shearing demonstration and a $500 cash prize for best market lamb. Bill Batty, a sheep man from Meaford, came down the first year with a superior Suffolk lamb that walked away with the big prize. The next year he won again. The third year, I heard Bill wasn't coming and I called to ask why. "You make people mad if you win too much," he said gruffly.

That surprised me. Bill didn't look like the sort of person who worried much about offending anyone. He was short and sinewy, with the wary expression of a man who has spent years trying to keep his temper under control.

"You're just raising standards, and what's wrong with that?" I said. Bill gave me that look that translates as "You're new here, aren't you?" Anyway, he wouldn't budge. So I asked him if he would come back and be my sheep judge. He shrugged and said, "Okay."

I learned more in twenty minutes watching Bill judge a pen of sheep than I did all year in my own barn. He took a sheep apart, looking into its mouth to judge teeth, under its eyelids to judge parasite load, up its fundamental orifice for God knows what. His life was devoted to the search for a practical, meat-producing sheep that could live on snowballs and fresh air. That made him a fierce critic of the purebred industry and its beauty pageants in the show ring. Bill believed the whole point of sheep farming was to produce crossbreds that would fatten on grass—a feed you didn't have to pay for and something a sheep could gather on its own. To do this you needed superior genetics, and Bill achieved it by ferocious culling.

"Look at those teeth!" he would growl, looking at a two-year-old female. "She won't live five years with teeth like that. Look at those hocks! You get sick of the sight of them waddling around the barnyard, half lame. Fire her out of here!"

He had a bad heart, and when he had judged enough, he would sit on a bale of hay, right under the No Smoking sign, and smoke a cigarette. A woman in the next booth over complained. Unfortunately, the fair board had assigned this booth to a group protesting wind turbines. Coincidentally, Bill had just that week had a visit from the wind turbine company offering him six figures to put one up on his farm on Scotch Mountain, where his family had farmed since 1848. Bill and the anti-turbine activist were soon toe to toe in a heated and bizarre argument. The eco-warrior was determined to protect the natural beauty of this place from green energy. The seventh-generation farmer was livid that a "blow-in" would dare to stand between him and his right to profit from his reduced carbon footprint. For a moment it looked like Bill was either going to have a stroke or stamp off in a huff, and I would lose my judge. I finally managed to steer Bill around to the hospitality tent, but the sheep committee had to work double shifts keeping Bill and the Wind Woman at opposite sides of the barn. By the end of the day I was exhausted. As they went out the door, both Bill and the Wind Woman declared that they'd had a great day and thoroughly enjoyed themselves.

Remembering those two locked in combat in the sheep barn reminds me that good people must always be given the chance to say what is on their minds, hear arguments from the other side, rebut them and pose fresh ones. It might seem endless and fruitless at times but, without a proper hearing, the shouting never stops, positions harden to stone and the search for common good always comes up empty-handed.

The antidote and softening agent for all sharply held convictions is the Canadian winter. Eventually, all but the most rabid zealots yield to the relentless pressure of hard frost, howling winds and months of isolation. The longer you stay up here among these drumlins, the less doctrinaire you become about things that don't really matter. You begin to notice that animals are much tougher and more resilient than you ever imagined. A horse, for example, is a cold-weather animal, built to live outside on the north side of a drumlin with its bum to the wind. Horses don't care for barns all that much because high winds make barns creak and groan, noises that make a horse anxious. Warm barns sound lovely, but they are a petri dish for every bug in the country. And for an animal whose standard reaction to everything is "Jeez, let's get out of here!" a barn can be suffocating.

THE GLEANER

࿉

Many years ago, my wife picked up a cast-iron hand-cranked corn sheller at an auction, just about the same time my neighbour Bill passed over his cornfield next door with his John Deere 4400 combine. I noticed there were all sorts of intact corncobs lying on the ground at the corners of the fields where the machine turned sharply, so I went out with an empty grain bag one Saturday morning and, in the space of twenty minutes, gathered as many cobs as the bag would hold. As chance would have it, Bill drove by in his truck and gave me a puzzled look, so I made a point of visiting the same day to explain myself.

"Not a problem," said Bill. "But you look so desperate!"

Gleaning after the harvest never really caught on in this part of the world, and by the time I had run that bag of corncobs through the hand-cranked corn sheller I began to see why. Forty-five minutes of cranking converted one bag of cobs into a 2-gallon pail of grain corn, which satisfied the hens for about two days. A minute with the calculator indicated that I would have to spend three 40-hour weeks gleaning and shelling to feed the hens all year. The savings to me at the prevailing market price of $3 a bushel would amount to roughly $75, or $1.60 an hour for my time. Even a freelance writer, putting in two naps a day and a long lunch at the diner in the village, can out-perform those numbers.

Another neighbour, Mike, remembers using one of those shellers for his mother's hens. But he shook his head when he saw me grinding cobs into a pail.

"Either get the boys to do it or shut the door on the barn so the neighbours can't see you. They'll be putting a tag day together for you before you know it."

One year, Bill and his brother were combining the cornfield next door and running a grain buggy back and forth to a transport truck out on the road. The next morning I noticed there was a small pile of corn sitting in the middle of the road with five crows standing on it, so I went out with a broom and a shovel and filled three bags. Ten minutes later Bill drove by, stared at the spot and drove on. Again I visited.

"Oh," he said. "That was you? I didn't think the crows would eat it all."

"Did you want it back?" I asked.

"No," he said. "I was worried some motorbike might slip on it and sue me. If you want some more, we had an oops! moment out there last night in the dark. The combine jogged right, but Roger went left with the buggy. It was maybe ten seconds before we saw it, but we left a pile of corn out there. You're welcome to it."

That afternoon I went out with the boys and gathered twenty bags off the field with a broom and a shovel. Bill saw all the bags and nodded approvingly. "When that combine sneezes, it feeds a writer's chickens for a winter."

A single John Deere X9 combine, operating through a normal growing season taking off 20,000 bushels a day, can harvest the equivalent of Britain's entire annual grain crop in the time of Henry VIII.

And what took a merchant navy to move it around could fit into one modern container ship.

The Five Books of Moses, which guide Christians, Jews and Muslims alike, offer explicit rules on the subject of gleaning. Leviticus 9:19 advises farmers not to harvest the corners of their grain fields or gather the gleanings in their vineyards. This food is to be left for "the poor and the stranger." Japanese Buddhists use the term *mottainai* to indicate regret at the waste or misuse of something sacred or highly respected, such as religious objects or food. Every culture has some "waste not, want not" pronouncement on the need to share the harvest with those less fortunate.

On our sideroad the farmers look after poor, strange artists like me and keep us on their cell phone contact list in case of emergency. In return I pay it forward, taking all my surplus eggs to the women's shelter, where I am known not as a writer, but as the Egg Man.

THE END OF THE WORLD
IS NIGHISH

෪

Many people move to the countryside out of a gnawing feeling that cities may collapse at any moment and the food supply will dry up. But moving a mere two hours away from the city is no guarantee of safety when food is scarce. As Lenin said, "Every society is three meals away from chaos."

One young couple said to us: "We want to be able to grow our own food, in case anything happens." To their credit, they had moved to a little acreage on the edge of town, not a cave in the mountains stocked with tinned food and ammunition. They were just trying to be a little more self-sufficient, and it's hard to argue with that. But you could see they shared a dread of a serious disruption to our way of life and were trying to protect themselves.

Every three or four years the *Globe and Mail* writes a truly depressing piece on the death of the family farm. The last one listed some alarming facts: while the value of land, buildings and equipment has skyrocketed, the price of wheat is exactly where it was in 1980. The average Canadian spends only 11 percent of their income on food, and the number of farm operators has dropped to less than 1 percent of the population. The article ended with the gloomy prediction that with driverless everything coming soon, "We will no longer have any farmers at all—only 'food production.'" The reader was left with the uneasy sense that a precarious system could come crashing down at any moment.

This same newspaper runs an article about the death of Canadian theatre just as often as they mourn the passing of the family farm. Theatres are closing, actors have no work, we have no standing on the international scene. You would think that after a half century of supervising this death watch on the family farm, as well as the theatre, book publishing, the nuclear family, small business, the climate and the economy, all of these subjects might at least have the decency to die. But they just won't.

The *Globe* article on farming came out just before the pandemic hit. Oddly enough, the one part of the economy that was virtually untouched by lockdowns was the farm. Farmers climbed into their tractors as usual that season, planted crops and harvested them without any hiccups. Other than price hikes, it was business as usual.

Last year my kids gathered at the dinner table using FaceTime to celebrate a birthday party, and for the first time I heard them agree they weren't interested in trying to buy a house because they all expect the planet to shake off the human species like a bad cold over the next forty years. I was caught flat-footed by this quiet acceptance of the coming apocalypse. But my wife pointed out that the two of us have not had to sit through as many depressing lectures on disappearing species, melting ice caps, dwindling forests, rising carbon levels and general climate gloom as they have. You really can't blame them for taking the dark view.

I remember being pretty nervous about the state of the world as a young man. I grew up with the atom bomb, acid rain and stagflation.

My parents were also gloomy about the future of mankind. They grew up during the Great Depression and a world war. My grandfather Arthur Goulding graduated from medical school the year of the Spanish flu epidemic. He ruined every dinner party for the next sixty years with his lectures on the inevitable pandemic to come and the collapse of world food supplies.

As a rule humans tend to think of their own time as the worst the world has ever seen. Perhaps the record for bleak thinking was reached during the 1300s when Europe moved into the Little Ice Age. Cooler temperatures were a shock to people who had become accustomed to the balmy conditions of the Medieval Warm Period. Several centuries of ideal weather had brought vast new acreages of marginal land into production, the food supply tripled and so did the population, which was lulled into a relative state of calm. When temperatures suddenly dropped and crops began to fail, the food supply shrank while the number of mouths to feed remained the same. The famine of 1315–22 killed six million people, and a lot of the survivors decided that the world must be coming to an end. Doomsday images appeared on the walls of every church in the land. Then the Black Death struck. People were so ground down physically and mentally by that point they barely had the energy to fight back against a plague. By 1360 Europe had lost somewhere between a third and a half of its population. An artist named Dürer would soon draw a picture of the Four Horsemen of the Apocalypse.

But the world did not end. Astonishingly, agricultural output recovered completely within just ten years, and by 1370 Europe began an economic rocket ride that, in spite of several notable interruptions, continues to this day.

As a writer I suffer from an incurable impulse to walk down the sunny side of the street and help people feel better about the world. Cheery worldviews get you excluded from most literary gatherings in this country. But I still think it's important to remind readers of the neighbourhood they live in and the voices of people who have passed through incredibly harsh times and still learned to watch for signs that things might be getting better. There is an old saying among sailors that the weather is a great bluffer ... and human society is a lot like that. The world has always seemed about to be engulfed by the tempest ... until suddenly it isn't.

During the online birthday party I reminded my children that it is never a good idea to put all your money on one square of the roulette wheel. By definition you only get one apocalypse, and humans have been terrible predictors of anything, let alone the end of the world. It's better to step back and take the long view, because you always come up against one indisputable fact.

Things really could be a whole lot worse.

Moving to the country won't guarantee a safe food supply anyway. On a trip to Cuba years ago I remember an old farmer telling me that he had given up trying to keep cattle because food was so scarce in the Special Period after the Soviets left that people would come out from the town in the night and steal any livestock he owned. "The only thing they didn't take was the beans. But the government was giving them beans, so I imagine they would have come for those too if the program for free beans stopped."

The Soybean Outlook Conference

ೞ

There's a line I love from Paul St. Pierre's *Breaking Smith's Quarterhorse* when Smith's wife suggests he do some reading to improve his skills and make the ranch run more profitably. He tells her, "Hell, I'm not running this place half as good as I know how to already."

I think of that remark whenever I face a crowd of arms-folded cash croppers and beef farmers gathered for the annual Soybean Outlook Conference sponsored by the local feed company. I've fought my way through blizzards to a hundred of these bun fights over the years, and they always fit the same pattern. The parking lot is crammed full of 4 × 4 pickups. Inside the hall a lineup of economists and agronomists wave infrared pointers at a screen to chart the way forward for a skeptical and very silent audience of mostly men. And I always assume the farmers are quietly muttering to each other that they already have far more information than they could ever possibly use.

My great-grandfather Walter Massey pioneered these gatherings in the 1890s by sponsoring hundreds of gala demonstrations in hamlets and towns across the country to mark the delivery of new Massey machinery. I wonder if he served grey roast beef, mashed potatoes, pale peas and pie as they do now at these late winter farm meetings. And I wonder if he asked a bank economist to tag along and predict where interest rates were going.

Progressive thinking is built into the farm population. The majority of Ontario's first settlers knew how to read and write, and they were quick to replace their log shanties with sturdy brick farmhouses. Legend has it that my own Loyalist ancestors brought a piano with them as they made their escape from Vermont in the 1790s. And they eventually sent their eldest son, Daniel, back to Vermont years later to ensure he got a proper education. I grew up with a generation of farmers who fought fiercely with their dads about the idea of growing soybeans, a crop most of the older generation had never heard of and didn't recognize as food. Over the course of a decade soybeans went from zero acres to the leading crop in Ontario. But it required a lot of people to change their minds about the way they would live. Many families left the farm, and the ones who stayed had to learn to live without neighbours. As the population declined, the useful stores on the main street closed and were replaced with tattoo parlours and pawn shops. We're lucky that our area is scenic, close to water and only two hours from the city. The old rural economy has been replaced by an eclectic mix of businesses serving mostly urban refugees.

Farmers are one of the last groups in our culture who have the luxury of changing their lives by changing their minds. If you work for any one of the organizations up at the podium leading the discussion about interest rates and end-of-year stocks for all the commodity groups, you are probably locked into a career path that is dictated by all sorts of forces beyond your control. This rule applies to a huge number of occupations today, from salaried teachers and civil servants through the professions to pretty much anyone who relies on one organization for a paycheque. You can decide to stay or leave that company or that line of work, but beyond that you pretty much have to go with the flow. And if you do decide to jump ship, your departure won't come up in conversation in the staff lunchroom after a week has gone by. But the farmers in the audience have a much wider range of options.

Obviously farmers face a host of forces beyond their control, but they do get to make an equal number of decisions about how to cope with those forces. They make decisions almost every day about when to plant and what to plant, when to buy and when to sell, when to expand and when to pull back. They can decide to use the land for something new or pull up stakes and try somewhere completely different. Very few people have those choices anymore.

And then there's the neighbourhood. Very few of us go to work in the same place where we grew up. Farmers go to school together, they make friends and watch each other's families find their way in and out of this way of life. There may be a tiny number of them, but the neighbourhood is still there, built on the foundations of the old rural community and still knit together by hockey and ham suppers. I think sometimes they take for granted a privilege that much of society has learned to live without.

And what do the agronomists and the economists think will happen next year to crop prices and interest rates? Not that much, as it turns out. Not surprisingly, the same answer they gave us last year. Things will go along as usual until suddenly they don't, and nobody has any idea when or if that will happen.

Then the meeting breaks up and the crowd moves slowly to the lunch buffet tables. Gradually the silence is replaced by a hum of conversation, and the hum builds to something louder as the visiting really gets going. By the time I leave the room the food is gone but the farmers are still standing in clusters, yakking about everything except what soybeans or interest rates might do. They're telling stories and making each other laugh and they're in no rush to get anywhere in particular. And you know they'll be back again next year because it's a great day out.

And I walk out through the lot full of big trucks to find my little car, and it reminds me that the real purpose of a farm truck is to find another farmer, after all.

THE POLITICAL LIFE
OF FLYOVER CANADA

ॐ

A glance at the electoral map the morning after the last few federal elections shows that the Liberal red tide may have engulfed the cities, but Conservative support remains strong and unchanged in the countryside.

I was born on a tree-lined street in North Toronto, the middle child of artists who were freethinking, socialist, pacifist, Volkswagen-driving, tree-hugging NDP supporters. If we had stayed put in the city, chances are I might have followed in their footsteps.

But as a child of six I was transplanted into a community of heavily armed Presbyterian cattle farmers who thought trees were noxious weeds. For some reason, probably the usual adolescent male fascination with explosives and dangerous machinery, I drifted away from the beliefs of my parents and let those farmers shape the way I look at the world. At the age of twenty-six I shocked my mother by putting on a blue suit and going to work as a speechwriter in the Conservative government of Bill Davis at Queen's Park in Toronto.

I came to my conservatism literally through the back door. Late one night, when I was sweeping up at the office of the weekly newspaper in Shelburne where I worked as the editor, the campaign manager for the new Conservative candidate tapped at the mailroom door and asked if I would be interested in writing material for the campaign. The next night I drove over to campaign headquarters, located in the old Thomas Funeral Home building in Alliston, and introduced myself to the candidate, George McCague. The backroom smelled of formaldehyde. It struck me as an inauspicious place to launch a political career.

I said, "How do you know I'm a Conservative?"

"I don't," answered George. "I hope you'll vote for me, but right now I need a writer more than I need a Conservative."

It was hard to resist someone who talked like that. George had wrested the nomination away from the longest-sitting member of a legislature anywhere in the British Commonwealth, the Reverend Canon Wally Downer, who defeated George's father to win the nomination for Dufferin-Simcoe in 1937. The farmers of the north half of that riding had been sending Conservatives to Queen's Park in an unbroken streak since Confederation. The closest they ever came to electing a Liberal was the year I worked on the Conservative campaign. George won the election of 1975 by the narrowest of margins. I followed him for the next five years, all the way back to the city and into the carpeted corridors of power. George was the man who taught me how to think, and I've been a small-c conservative ever since.

It's been getting harder. I start most days Conservative but by the time I go to bed I'm something else. The experts tell us that Donald Trump got elected because older middle-class white males from the flyover states were angry about government's failure to address the problems in their lives.

That made me think ... Grumpy old middle-class white guys who live in the country? That sounded a lot like me. Have I become a Trump supporter? I didn't think so, because I believe a society must remain civil if it hopes to remain a civil society. Is that all a Conservative can be these days?

The original definition of a conservative was an Englishman who was opposed to the idea of removing James II from succeeding to the British throne. Tory was an Irish word meaning "outlaw," and it was used to lambaste any supporters of James II. The Tories learned to call their critics Whigs, a Gaelic word for a Scottish outlaw. Studying political science at university, I learned that a conservative could also be someone who is cautious about change and anxious to hold on to those things that are deemed to be good. That idea appealed to me, and I carried it with me as I did constituency work for George. I learned very quickly that farmers are skeptical people who are not swayed by an elegant phrase or a flashy new idea. I already knew they were tolerant people, because they had been tolerating me for quite a few years by that point. And they were split down the middle on every issue, whether it was the wheat board, supply management or free trade, just the same way people choose sides in the city or anywhere else on the planet.

Today the grumpy old white guys I know are mostly successful people from other professions who should be delighted with their place in the world. The last fifty years have been extremely generous to them, and yet they walk around talking as if the socialists have burned their villages and carried off their women. They haven't earned their grumpiness any more than my children have earned their pessimism.

George never forgot that nail-biter election of 1975, and he always said to me, "You can't win this riding without a few Liberal votes." He made it a rule to be civil and not to antagonize a Liberal or anyone else if he could help it. He stayed in office for four terms and served another twelve years as the mayor of his hometown. Even my socialist mother voted for him.

At his funeral the church leaflet carried a passage from scripture that summed up his view of public service: "Like good stewards of the manifold grace of God, serve one another with whatever gift each of you has received."

Nothing at all grumpy about that.

There's another George who is probably the most famous example of a farmer-turned-politician. George Washington reluctantly left his sprawling plantation overlooking the Potomac River to command the Continental Army for seven exhausting years in the American Revolution. (My ancestors on both sides fought against him and so began journeys that eventually led both families to Canada.) Washington got walloped in sixteen battles over that time, but he kept his army together and won the very last engagement of the war at Yorktown and so emerged as the hero and leader of the new nation. He promptly shocked the world by going home to his farm and leaving the task of government to someone else. He only managed a few years out of the spotlight before he was hauled back to the capital to serve as the nation's first president.

Washington liked to give the impression he was wealthy but, like most farmers, he was land-rich and cash-poor. He complained that the only financial instrument that had held its value during the Revolution was the mortgage on his farm. He was so hard up that in 1787 he had to borrow five hundred pounds from a friend to make the trip to New York to be sworn in as president.

Washington is often compared to the Roman statesman Cincinnatus, another farmer who reluctantly responded to the country's plea for him to take charge of a chaotic government. A statue of Washington by the French sculptor Jean-Antoine Houdon in the rotunda of the

Virginia State Capitol shows him standing in front of a single furrow plough, wearing a determined expression that the sculptor managed to capture while watching the great man dicker with his neighbour over the price of a sheep.

When I worked for George at Queen's Park the whole building still ran on an agricultural timetable. When I arrived, workmen were busy scraping a century's worth of tobacco smoke off the ceiling of the legislative chamber, and the floorboards were still stained where members had missed the spittoons. There were lots of farmers on both sides of the House in those days. The high holiday for farm activism came in the middle of February when people from across the province converged in Toronto for three big events: the Cattlemen's Dinner at the Skyline Hotel near the airport, followed by the conventions for the Association of Agricultural Societies and the Good Roads gathering at the Royal York Hotel. Anybody who was well connected back home could spend ten days in the city, never more than a hundred feet from an open bar and a shrimp ring. The Pink Palace emptied out for a full week of glad-handing and promises and deal-making in the hotel hospitality suites. A good time was had by all, and the delegates eventually staggered home feeling better than if they'd won a Lions Club draw for a trip to Nashville.

Flash forward forty years and how things have changed. Farmers now make up only 1 percent of the population, and farm programs account for an even smaller portion of the budget. There are no votes to compete for anymore and no gravy trains to jump on. The vast network of farmer politicians that stretched from Windsor to the Ottawa Valley and north to the clay belt of New Liskeard has evaporated. We seldom see a farmer assume the reins of power, and they are sorely missed. Washington, Jefferson, Truman, Jimmy Carter and others left indelible marks on the North American body politic. In this country we owe a huge debt to people like E.C. Drury and Eugene Whelan.

People who work the land generally have a cosmic sense of what is enough, what will do. "We're building a fence here, not a piano," was the sentiment. This attitude would serve brilliantly in the public arena today, but the social network that used to launch those farmers into politics is gone.

Washington supervised a rowdy Congress as it hammered out a new constitution, and then he laboured another eight long years in the highest office to show people that democracy could work without descending into chaos. His teeth fell out and his strength ebbed away. When he finally escaped to "sit under his fig tree," he only got to enjoy two brief seasons at his beloved Mount Vernon. In the fall of 1799, he rode out in the rain to check his fences, caught a cold and fell into the hands of his doctors who finished him off by Christmas.

Washington probably went to his reward harbouring serious doubts about the future of both democracy and his own farm. I think he would be amazed to know that Mount Vernon is still standing today and surprised by the solution his successors came up with to make the place earn its keep. A group of women assumed control of the mouldering plantation house in 1858 and imposed strict rules of management. They reduced the property to 4 acres, turned it into a petting zoo and charged admission. Even so, the Mount Vernon Ladies needed donations from every state in the union to keep it afloat. The donations have been flowing for 160 years now, and Washington's "farm" remains pretty much as he left it.

But back to my own George.

He had been a municipal councillor and mayor in his hometown of Alliston for nearly twenty years by that point, the youngest warden that Simcoe County ever had, the founding chairman of the board of governors of Georgian College and the first chairman of the Niagara Escarpment Commission, but he still dreaded walking up to a podium or facing a camera. He would not read from a prepared text, especially when he was north of Highway 9, speaking to folks who knew him. He didn't want them to think he was getting above himself and reading government propaganda. So my job was to figure out how to get him more comfortable and help him find the right words for the occasion.

Part of the reason he lacked confidence is that he didn't think he was the smartest guy in the room. Most of the people he worked with had a better education than he did. George did enrol in the agricultural diploma program at the Ontario Agricultural College in Guelph. He always joked that everybody else needed two years to get their ag dip but he was done in half that time. That's because he failed his first year.

When we hear that a young man drops out of college, we naturally assume there was a lot of partying going on and he must have spent too much time at the pool table. But that was not the case with George. He loved school and he understood everything they were teaching him, well enough that his dorm room was always full of other students asking him to explain the difference between nitrogen and potash. But when it came to essays and exams, he couldn't get what was in his head down on paper. Today we would have called that dyslexia and given him an individual education plan. But this was the 1950s. When the marks came in, all the boys on the football team he'd been tutoring passed with flying colours, but George got 58.6 percent.

He called his father, Jack McCague, the owner of Glenafton Farms, one of the pre-eminent dairymen in North America and the first farmer in Canada to be named to the board of a chartered bank. George said, "Dad, I just need another 1.4 percent to pass. Could you speak to someone at the top?" And his father said, "I am at the top. I'm on the board of OAC and I won't do that for you."

And George said, "What am I going to do?"

And his father said, "You can come home and work for me."

He finished by saying words that should never come out of a father's mouth: "I don't think you're going to amount to very much."

George came home and went to work milking cows three times a day, doing tractor work in the fields and feeding the mink and the silver foxes in the fur ranch. I have read interviews where George claimed that he enjoyed working in the fur ranch, but I'm not sure how a person could enjoy chopping up dead stock. Ironically, he got a note in the mail from OAC the week after he got home saying he had won the Executive Award for all the work he had done with Junior Farmers and other voluntary groups at the college. He asked his dad if he could go back to Junior Farmers meetings and his dad reminded him that he was now one of ten employees and there couldn't be any special treatment. George went to the Junior Farmers anyway and made a point of working harder and staying on the tractor longer than anyone else.

He worked for his dad for two years, and in the summer of 1956 his father sent him over to a barn on Norval Kerr's farm, where he was to pitch loose straw from the mow down a chute into a baler. He was carrying a pitchfork and he went up the vertical wooden ladder with the fork in his left hand, grabbing each rung with his right as he went. One of the rungs was rotten and broke loose, he fell 15 feet and broke his back. He spent the next six months in a body cast that went from his ears to his pelvis and gave him that stiff posture he kept for the rest of his life. I once asked him if he did a lot of reading while he was bedridden, and he said he didn't spend any time in bed. In spite of the cast, he still curled and served as a very effective goalie for the floor hockey team. He even wrote a history of the Junior Farmers movement. He got married in the body cast.

By the age of twenty-five, George was dealing with two fairly serious setbacks: no profession and a serious physical disability. Most dairy farmers eventually end up with a bad back. It's not a good idea to start out with one. So George decided to go into real estate and insurance and eventually bought a sod farm. In 1958 he ran for Alliston Town Council, beginning a career in public service that would last for the next forty years. And he signed up for a dozen volunteer organizations in Alliston.

Back in 1937 Jack McCague had taken a run at the Conservative nomination for Dufferin–Simcoe against a young Anglican minister from Collingwood named Wally Downer. Jack was defeated. Thirty-eight years later, in 1975, George put his name up against the same man who had beaten his father, and he won the nomination and the election that followed. It was almost unheard of for a sitting member of the Conservative Party to be ousted in a nomination meeting. But Downer had served for thirty-eight years and promised twice publicly that he would retire before the next election. It's too bad Jack McCague wasn't alive to see that his son had clearly amounted to something. George arrived at Queen's Park having accomplished the one thing his father could not do. I believe at that point George became a free man.

The next year, George asked me to come to work for him full time. He was appointed parliamentary assistant to the treasurer, Darcy McKeough, who was Minister of Everything. So I became McNutt, the chief assistant to the assistant chief. I followed him around with the briefing books wherever he went, and we kept working on the speeches. Words were very important to George because he stood by them and staked his reputation on what he said. Once he got a phrase figured out that he liked, he would use it for the rest of his life. We would labour over sentences in his speeches as if we were writing out the Constitution for the first time. Sometimes he would take my notes to the podium and gaze at them for a very long moment, and my heart would leap at the thought that tonight would be the night he would read my speech. He never did. He would just tuck it into his suit pocket and start speaking off the cuff. Afterwards in the car he would apologize and thank me and remind me of the ideas and phrases from the text that he did use. And then we would go back to work on the next one.

George had no ambition past being the member for Dufferin–Simcoe. He didn't want to be premier. He didn't even care if he was in the Cabinet. He did want to be at the table, helping the room come to the right decision. The premier, Bill Davis, quickly realized how useful a man without ambition could be, and he used George as a mediator between the colossal egos at the Cabinet table. I lost count of the number of times Davis stood between two arguing ministers and said, "The two of you go into my office with George and whatever he agrees to will be fine with me." And I got to sit in on those meetings with my notebook, watching a skilled negotiator bring peace to the room and a decision back to the table.

George could solve problems that whole committees had been struggling with for months. I never saw him lose his temper or raise his voice at anyone in the five years I worked for him. He was completely colour-blind when it came to race, creed or gender. The government was still very much a man's world in those days and built on military foundations. But he treated everyone—women, young people, members of the opposition, union chiefs, environmental hotheads—with respect and unfailing courtesy. He didn't have much patience with partisan party politics. He would never attack an opponent. That's because he thought most people wanted basically the same things he wanted: a roof over their heads, meaningful work, to be treated with respect, opportunities for their kids. So scoring political points didn't make much sense to him. He always said during a campaign, "You can't win a riding without Liberal votes. Let's not talk about the terrible things they did or said. Let's just talk about the things we're going to do."

When you follow those instructions, a political speech becomes very short. Words must be chosen carefully. And no one will ever report that speech in a newspaper.

I was young and lost my temper all the time. The *Ottawa Citizen* ran an article referring to George as the "colourless member for Dufferin–Simcoe." He just laughed it off. "You're so emotional, McNutt. Would you rather they called me the colourful member for Dufferin–Simcoe?" he asked. "No, colourless is a good colour to be in this building."

I've written down many of the memorable things George said over the years and used them in my plays because I thought they needed wider circulation:

"A farmer is the only guy who can lose money thirty years in a row and then move into a big house in town for his retirement."

"A century farm sign generally means a hundred years without a single decent offer for the farm."

But there were serious things he said that stick in my memory:

"Good government is good politics."

"Don't assume the people on the other side of the table from you want to say no. Chances are that three of them are trying to figure out some way to say yes."

"Most people just want to be heard. Sometimes it's all they want. So hear them out until they are finished."

"Your personal opinion is not the most useful thing you bring into the room."

"We don't have to solve their problem, but we should explain to them the process and what their rights are."

"We'll never get them to vote for us, but maybe we can make them feel a little bad about voting against us."

He had great respect for the civil service, and they returned it. By the time he left in 1990, all sorts of people on both sides of the House were telling me they thought George McCague had one of the best minds at Queen's Park. Not bad for a guy with a grade 12 education who started out chopping up deadstock for the mink at Glenafton Farms.

A lot of people believe politics isn't the same as it used to be, but I'm not sure that is true. There was plenty of nastiness and betrayal in those days. The press was every bit as negative and lazy. The work was just as hard on family life, and there was precious little appreciation shown for the sacrifices people made. But there were also moments and voices of great civility.

George was a great fan of farmer thinking. He admired the virtues of resourcefulness, skepticism, tolerance and courage that came out of the old rural community on the Scotch Line where he grew up. His speech was peppered with phrases from the farm. He loved his community and laughed about its contradictions and complexities.

One day in 1977 he told me to take his car and drive up to Collingwood and talk to a farmer who had just written him a strongly worded letter of protest. He wanted the problem dealt with personally and right away, and he gave me very detailed instructions:

"I want you to listen to this man. Now, you may have to stand on one foot for an hour and then stand on the other foot for another hour. I don't want you to disagree with him or try to persuade him about anything. Just hear him out. And then come home."

I drove north and it was exactly as George had predicted. I stood outside the man's barn in a light rain for two hours until the man was thoroughly talked out.

In my report I said to George, "The guy makes a good point. He just wants to raise fifty turkeys, and the new marketing board requires him to buy quota for the birds. He says there should be some kind of an exemption for little guys like him."

George walked across the hall to the agriculture minister, Bill Newman, and got the exemption the same day. A few months later

I bought my own farm right beside that turkey farmer. George lent me $5,000 to help with the down payment. That farmer's name was Hugh McKee.

I might have stayed with George and thrown my hat in the ring when he retired ten years later. But the world was changing. The Conservative Party was attracting a strange new breed of young right-wing followers of Ayn Rand and toying with hard-nosed Republican tactics of the Reagan era south of the border. I wasn't sure I had any remarkable leadership qualities, but I did have a rodent's sense of when a ship was sinking. I left George and went down the street to take a position in public affairs for Canada Life, but I made a few attempts to stay connected. When Bill Davis retired in 1984 I started writing speeches for one of the leadership candidates, but I was uncomfortable when I realized the room always seemed to fill up with grumpy old white guys and very strange young men in ill-fitting white shirts. I asked one of them if he wore a white shirt because all the good colours, like black and brown, had been taken. He didn't get the joke, but I think my name went on a list.

One of the researchers from the premier's office confided to me that most delegates to the leadership convention fit the same profile: over fifty, male, white, wealthy and with both front feet in the public trough. The convention elected Frank Miller, a genial right-winger from Muskoka who was two years older than the outgoing premier. As NDP leader Stephen Lewis said, "They passed the torch in the wrong direction, to the previous generation." In the campaign that followed I heard the term "freefall" used for the first time. The Big Blue Machine's forty-two-year hold on the province was finally broken, and into the vacuum left by the exit of the progressives around Davis rushed an unsavoury mass of Amway soap salesmen who thought government should put up park benches, plant tulips and paint the *Bonaventure* now and then. I eventually withdrew to the countryside and dwindled into a party of one. Not surprisingly though, George won his riding handily and stayed in opposition for another two terms.

Elections are a blunt force instrument we use on the body politic to move it forward, much the way a mahout prods the elephant with a goad. Votes by themselves tell us almost nothing about who we are or what we think. One pile of ballots is simply higher than the other, and things change, usually quite slowly and incrementally. History is a series of zigzags.

The US zigs to the right and left with each election, lurching back and forth as it appears to toy with its own destruction. Each vote leaves us alarmed or slightly relieved, but the air is always charged with anxiety over what might happen next. The news headlines today are exclusively about that—what might happen next.

The election night of 2016 that gave Trump the presidency made me feel that rural people were on trial. A look at the American electoral map showed tiny urban blocks of blue surrounded by vast swaths of red. (That's what it looks like in Ontario too, if you reverse the colours.) The filmmaker Michael Moore claimed that Trump woke up a mob of uneducated white folks in the flyover states who mailed in a collective middle finger to Washington.

Except that he didn't. As the weeks went by, the media grudgingly began to accept that the country had simply shifted very slightly to the right, just as they shifted slightly to the left after two terms of George W. Bush and gave the nod to Barack Obama. In our elections in Canada we do much the same thing. In each example, voter turnout is low and the margins narrow. Politicians and the media are more polarized than ever before but there is no evidence that everybody else is. In fact the Stanford political scientist Morris P. Fiorina argues that the polling evidence shows that opinions in the general population cluster around the middle, rather than the extreme fringes. On balance most people agree that government should back out of our lives and learn to get by with less. But they have no idea how that should be accomplished.

"Everything is true and nothing is true," lamented outgoing president Barack Obama, quoting Albert Camus. Mark Twain observed that "a lie goes around the world and back again while the truth is lacing up its boots." That was literally true if you saw any of the fake news sites on Facebook from Macedonia.

New buzzwords refer to politics after 2016 as "post-factual," "post-truth" and even "post-reality." This is a troubling development and contributes more than anything else to our sense of worry that yet another sickness is about to creep across our border.

"Post-factual" is not a term likely to gain any traction in farming because there is no such thing as a post-factual chicken. There is also no post-factual way to deal with wireworms in soybeans. I'm sure you could find some website with a Macedonian address that will advise you to spread coffee grounds on the field and then do an interpretive dance in the moonlight, but our natural Canadian skepticism makes it unlikely any of us would act on it. When it comes to wireworms, we all tend to cluster in the middle.

Farmer thinking helps to explain essential Canadian characteristics: our basic decency, our skepticism and our tolerance. I like to think these qualities were born on the concession roads to people who knew that rugged individualism was not the best approach to a Canadian winter. No matter how rugged you are, you still need help when sickness strikes the house or your barn burns.

My wife's great-great-grandfather Charles Jack sailed from Scotland as a young boy on a leaky timber ship with his large family in 1853, landing in Hamilton in September. He walked behind a wagon pulled by two oxen to the village of Egremont on the edge of a huge tract of forest called the Queen's Bush. They cut their way 12 miles through thick woods to find their 400-acre tract, then hastily threw up a log cabin and dug in for the winter. They had to kill one of the oxen to survive that winter, and in the spring, Euphemia, his mother, took a fever and died, leaving her husband with nine children and an eight-month-old baby. Charles's father did not give up. He walked back out to Egremont and bought a horse. Charles remembered his father ploughing the first wiggly furrows between the tree stumps with the horse and ox harnessed together. Much of the farm lay underwater, and the first season Charles and his brothers were given shovels and put to work digging a ditch from one corner of the farm to the other. It took six years to complete that ditch, and when it was finished, three of the brothers left to fight in the American Civil War, saying they would rather be shot at than spend another season on that farm. Fifty years later one of the brothers wrote from California, remembering Proton Township as one of the "most damnable places in the world," overgrown with "adder tongue, cow cabbage, leeks and ground hemlock to no end ... " and the land under water six months of the year. Killing frosts ruined the first crops, and the family survived the winters on biscuits made from frozen potatoes and flour. "The cows ate better than we did," he said. The travelling preacher who was supposed to give the family comfort was so depressed he could barely get out of bed.

But the Jack family not only survived, they made history. Charles's sister married a McPhail and went to a farm a few miles north. The McPhails had a granddaughter Agnes who grew up preferring work with livestock to housework. Agnes never married. Instead she took up teaching and found her way into the farm cooperative movement and the United Farmers of Ontario. In 1919 the UFO swept to power in the downturn following the First World War, and two years later Agnes was nominated to run for the Progressive Party in Grey County for the first federal election in which women were allowed to vote. She won and joined the minority government led by William Lyon Mackenzie King, becoming Canada's first woman member of

Parliament. Over twenty years in Parliament as a Progressive and later as a founding member of the Co-operative Commonwealth Federation (the forerunner to the New Democratic Party), she helped lay the foundation for the modern welfare state, promoting pensions, employment insurance and universal health care and also fought against high tariffs that forced farmers to pay higher prices for machinery. Later, as a member of the Ontario legislature for East York (where my mother's family lived in relative comfort largely owing to high tariffs on farm machinery), she sponsored the first equal pay legislation in Ontario, introduced legislation as an ardent pacifist and pioneered prison reform. After an electoral defeat in 1951, she continued to be a voice for women, farmers, industrial workers, miners, immigrants and prison inmates.

The causes she fought for were inspired by her own experience growing up on a hardscrabble pasture farm along the Saugeen River in Proton Township. She knew what it was to struggle, and she worked all her life to make the struggle easier for those at the margins of society. She never made much money herself, and out of office she had to turn her hand to freelance work as a public speaker and correspondent for the *Globe and Mail*. She died in genteel poverty in Toronto at sixty-three, just before the Liberal prime minister offered her a seat in the Senate.

Her story reminds me that the national conversation in Canada may be driven by urban elites, but our national character has been shaped by people from the countryside. Two of my wife's relatives have Agnes McPhail's oval face and her distinctive high-pitched voice. One works as a 911 dispatcher in Simcoe County and the other as a nurse in the far north. Agnes would have been very proud of them both.

Pundits claim that because cities command the power to elect governments, the governments no longer need to listen to farmers. The urban–rural divide has turned into a canyon.

I believe this is a misreading of the results. There has been no great sea change in the way Canadians think or how they want to be governed. Given the option of sticking with the old faces or trying some new ones, they generally take the second route. Similarly, it would be a mistake for farm people to assume that the deck is suddenly stacked against them. Canadians are still a middle-of-the-road people. And there are plenty of subjects on which city and country people stand on common ground.

Food is a hot-button issue right now in the condos and suburbs. Hipsters and soccer mums think a lot about the safety, quality and ethics of food production and the distance it travels from farm to table. We can laugh about their obsession with backyard chicken huts and rooftop beehives, but behind the urbanites' fascination with stovetop maple syrup is an insistent need to know more about what they eat. That fascination can serve as a bridge between two solitudes.

Speaking of bridges, there are a few needed within the farm community itself. The Chicken Farmers of Ontario built one two years ago when they announced a 2,000-bird off-quota program for small producers of heritage birds. It was a small step that might reduce their stranglehold on chicken production by a fraction of a percent. And they gave up a part of the market they weren't interested in serving anyway. But at least the step they took was in the right direction. There are fewer than 1,200 chicken farmers under the CFO banner and something close to 30,000 backyard flocks and henhouses. If supply management wants to survive, it is going to have to figure out ways to prevent hobbyists from turning into lobbyists and enemies. The entry-level investment for young chicken farmers now stands at $3 million, which has prompted many critics to call for the dismantling of supply management. But busting up producer monopolies comes with its own risks. The supposed success story of New Zealand's deregulated dairy farms has come at the cost of ballooning farmer debt, water and air pollution problems and rising foreign ownership of the industry. China is now busy building a vertically integrated supply chain that threatens to keep milk prices low long into the future and drain profits away from the island nation. Economic nationalism is back on New Zealand's political agenda once again.

My children are always inviting their hipster friends from downtown Toronto to spend the weekend with us. I love the way they turn up in their lumberjack shirts and workboots, eagerly hoping to be asked to pitch hay to a horse or make soap in an open cauldron. Of course I don't make my own soap, and I don't own a horse. I'm not sure if I even have a pitchfork around, but I see the goodwill and respect on their faces and I do my best to give them a good experience and send them home with a few selfies doing useful farm work.

They are always so impressed by the skill set and resilience of country people, and they long for a piece of that world for themselves. They come back again and again, ready to pitch in and soak it all up. If it weren't for these kids, I would have given up square bales long ago. Now, because I don't want to disappoint them, I keep the old International 435 oiled up and under cover.

Their goodwill reminds me that the farm and rural spaces still offer a powerful narrative theme in Canadian public life. Even though that narrative no longer resonates in Ottawa or Queen's Park, we should not assume that it has lost its relevance. We should never assume that a countryman's words fall on deaf ears in the cities. Even in a city like Ottawa.

WHEN THE SPIRIT MOVES ME

༄

The chief purpose of a country property is to be looked after. I knew this as a young man, long before I bought my own place. When I was a student, my friends often invited me to join them for country weekends because they knew I was a willing worker and wouldn't flinch at the to-do list their parents presented at the breakfast table on Saturday morning. I found I was often stepping into the place that should have been filled by one of their own brood, someone who had phoned in sick at the last moment to avoid another weekend of forced labour at the "prison farm." The parents were usually alpha personalities, lawyers and bankers who enjoyed organizing work parties and barking orders. Mowing lawns and mucking out horses is painful enough work for a person with allergies. Being yelled at to boot is a tipping point for desertion.

I know that summer cottages have their work parties too. The May 24th opening and the Thanksgiving closing are command performances where attendance is strictly enforced. But that's it. The rest of the time is set aside for sunbathing and Trivial Pursuit.

A country property, on the other hand, always perches on the precipice of chaos. After a three-week absence, the jungle reclaims its own.

So when I bought Larkspur Farm in 1978, I made a vow never to make a chore out of the work and allow myself to become resentful of it. I would chip away at a thing until I tired of it and then give myself permission to down tools and do something else until the spirit returned. I did this for the first ten years until it became a deeply ingrained habit. It bothered the hell out of some people but, oddly enough, the same work habit helped me find a career as a writer.

Robertson Davies once observed that the problem with the humourist Stephen Leacock was that he suffered from a very strong work ethic. "He often wrote when it would have been better to sit still and wait for a good idea." I often tell my writing students that they are unlikely to get better at writing, but it is possible to get better at not writing. To do it you must first learn to conquer your wretched work ethic and willpower.

My wife took a while to climb aboard the train on this subject. She grew up on a farm where if a man was playing an instrument, riding a horse or firing a weapon over the bank at some distant target, he was said to be busy. As a result, no gate swung on a hinge, no vehicle started reliably and nothing had received a coat of paint since the Edwardian era. By nature Heath was impatient with the notion of waiting for the spirit to move a man. In the first years of our marriage she dragged me by the scruff back to the task at hand. But she has developed a grudging respect for the way I chip away at a thing without obsessing about finishing it. Over the years we have achieved a delicate balance: she likes to landscape with a riding mower and I like to repair broken machinery. We work as a team.

CHANGING YOUR LIFE
BY CHANGING YOUR MIND

૨૭

A lot of people in the modern world are locked into the way they live. They have a job, a boss, a mortgage and a lot of obligations. They live their way into a box, and it becomes very difficult to get out of that box. Oprah Winfrey made a brilliant career selling the notion that you can magically transform your life just by changing your mind. But for most people that is a cruel fantasy.

Farmers complain that they are at the mercy of forces beyond their control: weather, the vagaries of the market, input costs, disease and pests. But they still have more freedom to make decisions and act than most people I know. People who live in the country have a better chance of deciding what they are going to do today and tomorrow and next month and next year. Not everyone in the modern world can do that sort of thing, and we should be thankful for this privilege.

My neighbour Hughie, the apple farmer, pointed this out to me thirty years ago after I moved back to the farm. Hughie was delighted that he was living beside another person who didn't drive to work every day. Work was all around us, and we just puttered away at it. Personally, I found that once I took the commute and the meetings and the office traffic out of my day, my productivity soared. One day during that little window between the end of the haying season and the beginning of the wheat harvest, Hughie came over with his trumpet and a twelve-pack of beer at two o'clock in the afternoon. We sat in his truck in the orchard listening to Norah Jones while Hughie played along with his trumpet.

And Hughie said, "Who else on the planet gets to do this? Who can stop in the middle of the day without the boss telling them to get back to work?" Of course, we both did have a boss. It was a little voice in the ear that says, "Enough of that ... better get something done today."

Something there is that doesn't love a wall, that wants it down, said the poet. I would add that it doesn't love a two-stroke engine either or a water pump or any other moving part on a farm. If you need any evidence that the universe is cooling off, slowing down and wearing out, then you should come here for the weekend. After forty-two years I find myself surrounded by a mountain of repairs and unfinished projects.

The quarantine handed me the gift of unlimited time to finally get down to all this work and no excuse to slip into town or go back to the desk to meet a deadline. For the first time in four decades I finally got around to chores that normally slip away forgotten every season. I pruned and staked tomatoes before bottom rot struck, I installed a new washer on a garden tap that has dripped for ten years. The goldfish pond has a new waterproof coating. Shovels, axes, rakes and hoes have new handles. The apple trees are pruned. Three bush cords of firewood are stacked beside the house. Fifty meat birds and two pigs lie in the freezer. The henhouse even has a coat of paint. On any other occasion this would be called avoidance behaviour. Some writers I know have turned out two drafts of a novel in the same amount of time.

I read everywhere that the pandemic would change the way we live and work for a long time to come. I had my doubts about that, and sure enough, the headlong rush with all its noise and fuss has quickly returned. In the meantime I will remember the summer of 2020 as a very odd and productive blip that forced me to pause and smell roses … and get them pruned for once.

Death of Local Paper
Greatly Exaggerated

స

Staying in touch with people has been a priority on these sideroads since first settlement, and it has suddenly moved to the top of the list of urgent problems that need to be fixed. Local print newspapers are gone, no one watches TV news anymore, our radio stations serve tiny audiences and carry no news to speak of. Some of us have adapted to Facebook, which they say works fine for keeping informed. I rely on the telephone, which helps me stay in touch with my immediate circle but is useless for keeping me posted on breaking news on the sideroad. There isn't even a telephone directory to consult anymore. I often don't hear about a death in the neighbourhood for weeks.

It seems everyone in the country is struggling these days with their landline. My sister-in-law has had the same telephone line for fifty years, and the roots of a maple tree have grown right over it. Talking to her reminds me of the old days of the party line, when you had to shout to make yourself heard. You can always tell when the wind is blowing at her place because the phone cuts out completely after three minutes.

Bell's service people have been out many times to diagnose the problem, which is actually pretty simple. The cables are ancient and need to be replaced all the way back into town. But that isn't happening anytime soon because Bell's debt-to-equity ratios are in the same state as those of all the old carriers across the continent. They simply can't afford to fix the problem.

My line is no better. Static crackles over every conversation. Bell used to send a fellow out to check the relay box at the end of the road.

"Full of mouse nests," he would say, and the problem would get better for a few months. Then he retired and we learned to clear the mouse nests ourselves. Then the static became so loud that the mice moved out.

My friends ask why I don't just give up the landline and accept that cell phones are the way of the future. But I'm reluctant to do that for a very silly reason. You see, my number begins with 445, which dates me as one of the older residents of the community. My landline has the patina of old age and long service. In a community that sets rigorous standards for what constitutes a local resident, I like to think my 445 gives me favoured status.

There's certainly no other reason to be attached to this old phone. The service department is now in Mumbai. When I first moved up here in 1978 I shared a party line with four other families. The voice at the other end of the line often sounded like someone shouting at you across a ploughed field. We eventually gave up the party line to get the internet, a decision I made with great reluctance and now regret bitterly because I had to abandon the most reliable news service I have ever known—Kenny Jardine, the bachelor across the road. I shared a party line with Kenny Jardine for twenty-five years. He was joined at the ear to the widow Helen Kenwell up in Maxwell. Long before internet chat rooms, I could log on to The News with Kenny and Helen every morning just by picking up the phone. Traffic accidents, barn fires, marriage collapse, coyote predation, new equipment purchases ... Kenny and Helen were first with the news and free with their comments.

I gave up this useful and colourful free service in favour of the internet, which turned out to be a pale and lifeless substitute. Dial-up was obsolete the day it was hooked up. A version of high-speed finally came to us about ten years ago, but it still won't deliver a movie reliably on a Saturday night, and the news comes from every part of the globe except the Pretty River Valley, which is the only area of any interest to me. Helen and Kenny are both long gone now, and I have become dangerously uninformed.

When I was a boy on the farm we had twenty-six people on the party line. Information came out of that phone by the gigabyte. Our farm sat on the area code boundary between 705 and 519. You could make a free local call for 15 miles across the county to the east, but a call across the next road a mile west meant a long-distance charge. Two farmers on opposite sides of that road devised an ingenious system to beat the telephone company. They could each see the other's barn doors from their front yards, and they invented a semaphore code to send messages back and forth. Left door open meant "I'm coming to you." Right door open meant "You come to me." Both doors open said "yes." Both doors closed said "no." Both doors open and red flannel underwear hanging from the crossbar meant "Emergency! Get over here right away!" It will take that kind of creative thinking to solve the problem of telephone communication in rural Canada.

The old listening posts are still there. Some of us have not discovered how useful they are or learned to rely on them more often. There's the mailbox, the general store, the loading dock at the feed mill, the Driveshed Coffee Club, the nail salon and the church breakfast club. Some new ones are coming into their own: there are no fewer than twelve Probus Clubs that meet every month along this shoreline of Georgian Bay. City people assume that the farm truck was designed to carry stuff. Somehow they fail to notice that these trucks run around all the time with nothing in the back. That's because the chief purpose of a farm truck is to find another farmer. When you find one you get out and hook your elbows over the gunwales of the truck box and catch up on the news for an hour or so.

A friend of mine invested in a company that offered an on-farm seed treatment service on the prairies. Instead of loading the grain, driving it into town and waiting all afternoon for the mill to treat the seed with pink fungicide, a farmer could call this company and it would come and treat the seed on their own farm, leaving them free to do something else. All in the name of efficiency. The business failed in its first year and my friend never got his money back because the investors failed to grasp that farmers looked forward to the trip into town every bit as much as they looked forward to John Deere Days and the Soybean Outlook Conference. They tell their wives they are off to do something useful and then spend the afternoon in the Legion throwing darts and catching up on the news with their friends while the feed mill sprays the pink stuff on their grain.

When I worked for the local MPP in the 1970s there were fourteen weekly newspapers that served eight towns in the riding. Today only one survives in print form, the *Creemore Echo*. The rest all morphed into online versions of their former selves, including the two papers I edited in the 1970s. The major ones, two Thomson chain newspapers in Orangeville and Collingwood, used to occupy large buildings and employed dozens of people. Their editors and publishers were leading citizens. But both papers shut down more than ten years ago. The Collingwood building was converted to a dance and theatre studio, and the Orangeville building stands empty and abandoned. But there are still about a dozen or more newspapers online serving their local communities from behind paywalls. Everything has changed, but once again it really hasn't.

My papers, the *Free Press & Economist* in Shelburne and the *Citizen* in Orangeville, were run by the Claridge family, slightly eccentric newspaper people who served their communities for four generations. The patriarch, T.F.E. "Nice Day" Claridge, led the town band that played in the gazebo at the fairgrounds all through the summer.

The *FP&E* had been around since 1875, but the *Citizen* was the brainchild of T.F.E.'s grandson Tom Claridge and his partner Harry White, another Shelburne native who was a friend of my family since I was about eight years old. (Harry lived at our house in Toronto while he was taking a course to be a mortician. He cut our hair once a month, and I was always puzzled why he made us lie down on the chesterfield to do the job.) In 1974 Tom and Harry decided to take on the Orangeville *Banner*. Thomson newspapers were guided by a rigid order from on high: "Every page must pay." That meant every page was filled up to the 80 percent line with advertising, leaving only 2 inches for editorial material that often came out of the US. Tom and Harry thought Orangeville deserved a better newspaper.

I had just dwindled to a halt with my studies of economics at University of Toronto and was certain of only one thing: I had no future as an economist. Harry was at loose ends too. He had given up a sales job with a drug company, and he came to my mother's farm looking for my sister to see if she might run the front desk. Instead he found me surrounded by a collection of veal calves, pigs and ducks. He couldn't believe I was sitting there two courses short of a degree and working on a novel, which to him was the same as doing nothing. He offered me a job as a reporter for the *Citizen*. We opened for business in the Broadway Cleaners building on the main street right beside the Town Hall, with an editor whose name I have conveniently forgotten, because on the third day, the police came around and took him away. Harry turned to me with his eyebrows raised and said, "You took some English courses, didn't you?"

"I took one course in drama," I replied.

"That's one more than I've got," he said. "I guess you're the new editor."

I have a lasting picture in my mind of Harry the salesman standing by the front window in our new office in his crisp white shirt and tie, a coffee cup in one hand and a cigarette in the other. Absolutely nothing was happening—the phone silent, the hook that held the news columns empty and only flyers in the morning mail. With a shrug of the shoulders he would say, "I think I'll take a walk up the street and let a parking brake off. See if I can generate some news."

It was a trick to fill a sixteen-page newspaper with local news in a town of 7,000 people. There was a strong temptation to reach for the boiler-plate bulletins from the agricultural office warning about the advance of the alfalfa weevil or an uptick in warble flies on dairy cows. But our mission was to find items of local interest to show up the *Banner*'s lack of effort in local newsgathering. We had contests to think up the silliest headline for a town with no news. "Snow Falls on Broadway" or worse, "Still No Snow on Broadway." And, at twenty-three, I really had no opinions worth repeating for the editorial page. Fortunately, Tom had lots of those and fired them up to us from his office at the *Globe and Mail* in Toronto.

The first week Harry asked me to write a column to help fill the blank spaces on the editorial page. So I wrote out a title, "Letter from Wingfield Farm," and told a story about my sick duck. Over the next two years, Harry became the Dear Ed in the salutation. He read each column Monday morning, just a few hours before we went to press. If Harry smiled, I knew it was okay. If his brow furrowed, I knew the piece needed work. If he laughed out loud, I knew the readers would laugh too. There were plenty of opportunities to abandon the effort.

Like the time I made snotty comments about snowmobiles and had the Kinsmen Club and the small engine repair shop write irate letters demanding a retraction and telling me to go back to where I came from. Harry just laughed and complimented me on generating mail. The column eventually won a Best Column award from the Ontario Weekly Newspaper Association in 1976, which came with a $50 prize and an all-expense-paid train trip to Ottawa in the company of Tom's father, Fred Claridge, and Walter Walls, the publisher of the *Dundalk Herald*. I left the paper a few months after that but kept writing the column while I was working at Queen's Park. Then, in 1984, I gathered up the stories and fashioned them into a stage play, *Letter from Wingfield Farm*, and put it on at the Orange Hall in Rosemont. So began the saga of what is now the longest-running series of stage plays in Canadian theatre history.

Fred Claridge never tired of telling me, "Names are news, Danny. Every name you put in the paper sells five copies. The mother to that name, the aunts, the grandmothers, all of them will buy a copy to see that name."

During my time at the *Citizen*, the town clerk, Bob Lackie, took me up to the second floor of the Town Hall to show me the old theatre, which had not been used since 1930. The room was filled with dust-covered cardboard boxes full of tax records. Twenty years later the town restored the theatre, and *Letter from Wingfield Farm* came back home to appear on a real stage. I went on to write fourteen more scripts for that theatre. The Orange Hall, the *Citizen*, Theatre Orangeville and the residents of Dufferin County together would prove to be the launching pad and cheerleaders for a young playwright and propel him to a professional career in the theatre.

The *Citizen* was printed in Shelburne by a joint-partnership company in a steel building attached to the rear of the old blacksmith's shop that housed the *Free Press* offices. The business was still using an ancient hot-lead linotype machine from 1914 for its commercial printing work and an even earlier rotary press that had printed the first issues of the paper in the 1870s. In the same row of machines was the new Compugraphic phototypesetter that Tom had just purchased. In bad weather, snow would wisp in through the cracks in the floorboards and collect inside the Compugraphic and cause shorts. Fortunately, the machine came with a limitless supply of fuses, and I would sit on the floor replacing each fuse one by one until the lights came back on.

That row of machines along the wall of the *Free Press* offered a snapshot history of community newspapers from first settlement to the present day. The early hand-operated rotary presses using hand-set type were cheap to buy, and anyone could start a newspaper and grind out a few hundred copies every week. In its early days Orangeville boasted no less than five papers, all single-sheet publications. Then the hot-lead linotype machine invented in Baltimore in 1884 allowed one operator to compose 6,000 characters per hour, three times the speed of a compositor setting type by hand. The linotype was a much bigger investment for the owner, but it helped produce a bigger, better newspaper, and it forced smaller competitors out of business. The industry consolidated until web offset printers and phototypesetting in the 1970s reopened the field. Soon every town had competing news-papers again. Then desktop publishing and the internet appeared, creating a perfectly level playing field that allowed anyone to start up a newspaper for the cost of the software. The only drawback was fig-uring out some way to get the reader to pay for it. Today there are at least fifteen online news services, each one aimed at a particular town or village.

The only constant over two centuries for local newspapers in small-town Canada is that no community will go for very long with-out one. Somebody will eventually find a way to fill the need for police and fire reports, hockey scores, lost dogs, auction sale notices, Santa Claus parade pictures, town council and school board meetings. And names will always be news.

If You're Coming Sunday, Bring a Hot Dish

ॐ

As an economics student I was required to read Thorstein Veblen's *Theory of the Leisure Class*, which introduced the concept of conspicuous consumption for the first time. Reading Veblen is like driving to Kenora in thick fog. The book tied my head in knots until I read a critique of it by H.L. Mencken much later. Mencken noticed that the professor had taken a page and a half to observe that Anglicans go to church not because they are afraid of the devil but because they like the music.

If Veblen had said just that I might have read further, because I was raised Anglican and it was the music that kept me going to church. I sang as a boy soprano at St. Clement's on Duplex Avenue in Toronto every Sunday through the winter. I learned all the hymns, the psalter, many anthems and once had a go at the solo voice in Allegri's *Miserere Mei*. (I was benched in favour of another soprano who could hit the high C reliably.) Our choir even made it to the stage at Massey Hall. My mother drafted us all into her little choir at St. Luke's in Rosemont every summer and made us attend Sunday school in the basement, taught by an elderly Welsh farmhand named Tom Pate who had the oddest way of spinning scripture. "Do not judge by appearances," he read to us from John 7:14, and then told a story about a man who came to Rosemont and everybody thought he was a good person at first. It turned out he wasn't, so Tom warned us we should be careful about new people. At age ten I was pretty sure that wasn't what John had in mind when he wrote that passage, but I was also conscious of being a new person myself and felt the eyes of the class on me.

The part I liked most about church in Rosemont was the twenty minutes of visiting after the service on the lawn out front with the traffic whizzing by on the other side of the hedge. It was all part of a tradition that included basement suppers across the street in the Orange Hall and presentation dances for young couples upstairs with the Price Family Orchestra playing waltzes and foxtrots while the men leaned on car hoods out in the parking lot drinking rye out of stubby Coke bottles. I toyed with the notion of becoming a minister myself and doing pastoral care to the community I had adopted and come to love. But even as a teenager I realized the church was an institution in steep decline, and I couldn't make up my mind if I was there for the faith, the music or just the girls. Years later Heath and I came back to St. Luke's in Rosemont to be married and then went looking for a new church near my farm where we could introduce our children to the same sort of experience I had known.

Several members of my extended family were church people. My grandmother's brother Denton Massey was one of the great orators of his day. He founded the York Bible Class in 1933 with eighteen people at the first meeting. The class grew by leaps and bounds until he filled Maple Leaf Gardens two years later with an audience of seventeen thousand young people and another twenty thousand standing outside on the street trying to get in. Denton's preaching was carried on radio and reported in *Time* magazine and created a following that swept him to victory the next year as the federal candidate for Greenwood in East York and made him a key contender for the Conservative Party leadership in 1938. He could easily have been prime minister. But Denton had a very short attention span, a knack for saying the wrong thing privately and absolutely no idea how to handle money. He quickly racked up a new record for absenteeism in the House of Commons. He managed to win a second term because he was out of the country during the war for both elections and wasn't around to remind his fellow Conservatives that he was actually a socialist. When he got back he was soon defeated, and after a brief flirtation with car sales became an Anglican priest.

Uncle Ba, as the family called him, was a real spellbinder. I had been brought up to believe that no sinner was ever saved by a sermon longer than ten minutes. But Uncle Ba had stamina. He came to Lakefield College School in 1965 and preached a fiery sermon to us: "Are You a Clock with No Hands?" Of course, he had a prop—a big alarm clock with no hands. It seems completely ridiculous to describe it now, but we were all fervent Christians by the time Uncle Ba sat down an hour later. We were eager converts ready to devote our lives to good works. The effects wore off after a few hours, and we were ourselves again by morning. But I had felt the power and the glory of a good tent meeting firsthand.

My grandfather professed to be agnostic, unless he was in Uncle Ba's company, at which point he became an atheist. He was coldly dismissive of all sermonizers and "soap salesmen," as he called them. My mother's faith was a total mystery to me, although she said the prayers and recited the confession in a penitential voice that she used nowhere else in her life. I once took Heath and Mother to Savannah, Georgia, where we attended Sunday service at the Black church in the historic quarter of the city. With a big choir and a band playing, it was all very boisterous and athletic. Soon Heath was standing on the pew on one side of me singing and swaying with the rest of the congregation. On the other side my mother sat knitting in silence and at one point leaned over to say quietly, "I believe the road to salvation begins with self-control."

When I had my own young family I took them up to the Anglican Church of the Redeemer, a pretty little brick building where Heath's parents had been married in the 1950s by the same Reverend Wally Downer that my friend George later forced out of office at Queen's Park. I advanced in church work over the years to become the People's Warden and then the Rector's Warden, roles that reminded me, like the smart rap of a cattle cane over the snout, that I had limited gifts as a leader. The Church managed to come down on the wrong side of just about every difficult issue of the day and battled furiously about everything from gays in the clergy to the cost of photocopying. Finally I realized I was there, as Veblen said, for the music. And maybe for the visiting at the breakfasts after the service and the fact that, in winter-time, the church hall offers just about the only flat surface where young children in the countryside can mill about freely with their coats off. Then I read somewhere that at the current rate of attrition, the Church would be down to its very last Anglican by the year 2050. That would make me ninety-nine years old and probably that last Anglican they were talking about. I drifted away from the flock.

My little church has continued to dwindle since then, but there are lots of new, spacious churches in the area with vigorous Sunday schools and crowds of young people. In a secular age, where most of the population describes themselves as "Other," there are still more than thirty churches in town and the surrounding township, more than ever before in our history.

In 1984 I was pressed into service at the last moment as a pallbearer at Uncle Ba's funeral in a little church on Huron Street in the Annex in Toronto. It was the only funeral I have attended where there weren't enough men in the congregation to carry the coffin—just five of us, including the funeral director. It was saved from being a completely depressing affair by the Four Sisters of the Apocalypse, who came out in full regalia with their daughters. We went for a lovely lunch and visit afterwards in the Great Hall at Hart House.

NAVIGATING THE
TOWNSHIP ROADS

꙰

I f you are looking for a pattern to the township road system, don't be surprised if you stumble across the meaning of life in the middle of your search.

I've been driving up over the escarpment on Highway 26 and Highway 4 since Lester Pearson was prime minister, and I know all the townships by their maiden names and nicknames: Amnesia, Euthanasia, Floatin' Proton, Flyspray. The roads used to go by names too, rather than numbers. There was a Hogback, an Old Mail Road, a Magnetic Hill, Back Lines, Blind Lines, Old Settlements and a whole bunch of Deviation Roads that for a long time I assumed was a Bob Dylan song or else a cautionary sign, like Beware Falling Rock. I have lived long enough to see amalgamations and restructuring give these little roads new designations that look more like a postal code than a road sign. The result is general confusion for anyone straying off the provincial highways into the gorse bush of the township network.

It seems every road now has three different names: there's the old name the neighbours have for it, there's another given by county and provincial engineers in the 1970s and then a third name or number assigned when Ontario premier Mike Harris introduced the concept of off-loading roads to lower-tier governments. I grew up within eyesight of the Sixth Line of Mono Township, which got promoted to Airport Road in 1968 and then County Road 18 sometime in the 1990s.

There is a pattern to all this, but it's a bit like Cronshaw's intricately woven Persian rug in the Somerset Maugham novel *Of Human Bondage*. The pattern is far too complex to be understood by mere mortals.

The problem goes all the way back to first settlement when, in 1830, Lieutenant-Governor John Colborne drew a sieve through the taverns of Yonge Street to staff survey crews that would mark out the Queen's Bush, the name given to the vast swath of forested Crown land stretching from Shelburne to Owen Sound. The crews used a variety of survey systems and did not visit with each other or share ideas. There are all sorts of theories why the crew that left Hall's Tavern at Wrigglesworth Corners in Shelburne set off at a 30-degree angle from the other guys doing Simcoe County. But that's where the Toronto-Sydenham Road (Highway 10) comes from, and it explains why the old townships in Dufferin and Grey appear to be cut on the bias. Melancthon was the only township in Upper Canada whose interior lot lines did not run parallel to the township boundaries. The story I like best says the crew was following a treasure map leading to a silver deposit near Flesherton.

Highway 10 was originally called Hurontario Street, so named because of a straight line drawn on the map in 1818 by a perfectly sober Sir Peregrine Maitland to connect Lake Ontario to Lake Huron. Maitland also gave names to many of the townships, on a whim naming Tiny, Tay and Flos townships after his wife's dogs. (He might just as easily have named them after his own dogs Spike, Luke and Big Red.) But the crews who tried to follow Sir Peregrine's imaginary line found themselves struggling through the thick forests, limestone cliffs and bug-infested swamps of the Niagara Escarpment. Eventually roads were built on most of the Hurontario line from Port Credit to Collingwood. It remains the name of the main street of both towns. But the road disappears in many places in between and becomes Centre Road in Dufferin County and Lavender Hill Road, Eighth Line and Highway 124 in Simcoe County. When the Toronto–Sydenham Road to Owen Sound was finally completed, thirty-nine taverns sprang up over a distance of 38 miles, making the trip more arduous than ever. Some people with the best of intentions never made it to Owen Sound.

There were five major survey systems used in mapping out Ontario with something like 166 variations, resulting in the crazy quilt we have today. Farm lots were measured out in long narrow strips called "string hundreds" in North Simcoe. In some townships concession roads ran north–south and were numbered sequentially. Elsewhere, like Dufferin County, the farm lots were square and the numbers started in the middle at a Centre Road or Baseline and went out both ways with an East or West tacked on to the number. Sideroads connect the concession roads east to west and go up by multiples of five in Dufferin County but have no pattern at all in parts of Simcoe and Grey. I have lived on Sideroad 30 31 for forty-four years, and if I were tied up and tortured with a hot poker I couldn't tell you what the numbers are for the roads north and south of me. They will always be the West Church and the Min Baker to me.

Google Maps is no help with any of this. It might help you get across the township to find another main provincial highway and get away, but it's hopeless at finding the people you are supposed to be having dinner with. How is it I share the same fire-code number with someone 9 miles south on the same road in the same township? (They turn out to be nice people and we exchange mail regularly.)

When I had a fall in the barn a few years ago and broke my hip, my wife had to talk the ambulance driver in by phone. Every time a new driver with Purolator brings a parcel to the house, he has to call for directions. That's because I have three addresses. There's one for Canada Post that will get my mail to Louise, the postmistress at the village store, who hands it on to Rob the mailman, who often brings it right to the farm so he can visit with my big Dexter dog. But if you type that same address into Google Maps it puts me 15 miles west in Thornbury or 11 miles south in Creemore. Then there's the township address that requires you to use the township name, not the village, and add the word "North" to my road. The garbage truck is supposed to use that address, but they often get lost and skip us altogether.

Given names on signs will eventually vanish from the road system entirely, just as they are being peeled off schools and statues are toppled. All human beings eventually irritate and offend someone, and it costs a lot to have the signs removed and replaced when they fall out of favour. Numbers and letters will prove to be much safer choices in the long run. In very old societies, like rural England, or the island of Barbados, there are no road numbers or signs at all. People give directions according to landmarks.

In the meantime if you want to know how to get here from there, the rule is the same as it always was. Ask the old guy at his mailbox. He'll tell you to keep going down the Blind Line until you see the flock of sheep on the road. That's our place.

CHAMPLAIN SLEPT HERE

ॐ

There is a legend among historians that Samuel de Champlain, the great mapmaker, explorer and arguably the first Canadian, spent the winter of 1615 in Huronia, the land of the tobacco- growing Petun people. I say a legend because it appears the great mapmaker was pretty much lost the whole time after he paddled up the Lachine Rapids into the Great Lakes. So some say it's also possible he spent that winter in Peterborough or the Finger Lakes district of New York. They're not quite sure. Champlain himself was quite certain he was in China.

That's what I love about history. You reap such handsome returns in conjecture for just a trifling investment of fact. I like the Huronia winter version because it places the old boy right next door to me and makes him a neighbour. And he was a blow-in, just like me.

There's something totally manic about Champlain. He crossed the Atlantic twenty-six times without losing a shipmate. On one occasion, the captain lost his nerve and Champlain took the helm, safely steering the ship onto some soft rocks and supervising the evacuation of the ship. No injuries were reported. He explored six provinces and ten states and founded the first post-Columbian European settlement in Canada. He did it on a wing and a prayer with other peoples' money and never found anything he was hired to look for: no China, no spices, no Northwest Passage, Fountain of Youth or gold.

His most important legacy was the term *métis*, a French word that means "mixed," which is what he thought we should all be, if we had any hope of living in peace. Four hundred years later, I think he would be very pleased to see how mixed Canada has become.

I look out my office window at the cornfield that hosted the village of Etharita in 1615, and I think of him resting on a pile of beaver pelts in a longhouse, telling lies and smoking the winter away as a guest of the Petun. They obviously enjoyed his company, and they handed him around like a pet turtle for about twenty-five years. They taught him to live off the land, and he suggested they stop sleeping on the ground, a simple innovation that doubled the lifespan of anyone he met.

It's true he did start a war with the Haudenosaunee, but his mistake was bringing firearms to the semi-finals of the lacrosse season. The result was tragic and set his *métis* program back by a century. He regretted his mistake profoundly.

For years my field has rotated between crops of corn, soybeans and wheat. In Champlain's day it was corn, beans and squash all planted together in little hills, a concept the natives called the Three Sisters. Sam talked about how easy it was to get turned around in the cornfields of the Petun, a significant admission from a man who was uncertain of his location pretty much from the day he stepped off his veranda in Brouage, in France. Nothing changed for him, and when he died in 1635 his gravesite was promptly paved over and forgotten. In death as in life, his whereabouts are unknown.

There's something about winter in the country that brings a person to heel and reduces life to simpler terms. E.B. White insisted it was a full-time occupation staying warm, fed and amused, so it must have been a special kind of torture for a spirit as restless as Champlain's. Or maybe it wasn't. He may have been happy to gather calories and rest up for the spring runoff.

There is a dramatic statue of him on Parliament Hill, holding his astrolabe aloft and sighting his position. He's holding the thing upside down, which is not surprising because he probably didn't use one. I like to think the statue captures him heaving the thing into the bush and telling his native friends to take him wherever the hell they wanted. He was in no rush to get anywhere and was looking forward to the trip.

As the snow retreats to my fencerows and a warm gust rattles last year's cornstalks, I imagine the great man scanning the skies for returning geese and packing his kit for the next adventure. It was nice to have him here. I enjoyed his company and his talk of courts and kings, the vast forests, high-flowing rivers and rough seas that lay between us and his home. It sure made spring come faster.

I hope he visits again someday.

FOOD IS THE BRIDGE

૨

I've been cracking jokes about the way farm women cook for decades now. I love to make sport of the Jell-O and Cool Whip salads with carrot slices and pink and green marshmallows. How have Bamby bread and processed cheese slices survived for a century without any attempt at reform? When will the ladies in the kitchen at the back of the community hall relax their inflexible rule that roast beef goes into the oven at the same time as the peas and that they both cook until they are grey?

I finally figured out the crumbling beef and pale peas tradition by watching Heath's mother cater to her extended family in her enormous farm kitchen. She told me that food was dangerous and could kill you. The oven was the place you put food to make it safe. Once you understood this, it became clear that heat was love, and the more heat you put into dinner, the better it was for everybody.

"Dinner," of course, is incorrect. I had to be trained to refer to the meal at the end of the day as "supper." Dinner comes in the middle of the day. And lunch happens at midnight after the dance at the hall or when guests have stayed late in your kitchen playing the accordion and arguing about supply management.

Heath rounded on me about the rural menu fairly recently. She said, "You forget that for a very long time, there were no fresh vegetables at all between November and May. We didn't get lettuce from California. We were lucky to see an orange. Those canned fruit salads you find so amusing were the only source of vitamin C we had."

Of course, she has a point. All the fresh fruit and vegetables came in a rush in July and August, and the surplus went into Mason jars on shelves in the basement. Mustard pickles, corn relish, jams, jellies, stewed tomatoes, rhubarb, plums. Bags of potatoes, onions and turnips were stored in the root cellar, and there was a pile of clean sand to bury the carrots and protect them from frost. Even eggs were pickled because the hens stopped laying in the dark of winter. I went to a farm auction sale in 1990 where the couple told us that they stayed in the farmhouse all winter except for a single run in February to restock staples like rice, sugar, tea and coffee—which were the only edibles they couldn't grow on the farm. That was only thirty years ago, but Heath nodded her head and said that was how she remembered it too.

She was raised on a cattle farm in the sand hills of Mulmur Township where the girls spent every late afternoon after school with hoe in hand, hacking weeds out from between turnips and onions. If they were very, very good they were allowed to go out for a treat ... as soon as the carrots were hoed and the tomatoes were staked.

If you want your children to develop a love of gardening, never put them to hard labour at an early age. Heath has two callused spots just below her kneecaps from all that weeding on hard ground. "Just like a goat," she says crossly, rasping them down with a foot-long file. She learned to love July and August, when the ground baked to concrete and nothing would grow, not even a weed. Then she could escape out to the hayfields with her sisters and throw square bales of hay. Her father appreciated the help he got from his girls and said he couldn't have kept the farm going without them. Despite the heat and the thistles raising a rash of welts on her arms and the backbreaking work, Heath remembers the relief of being able to stand straight on the hay wagon with the sun on her face and the breeze in her hair. Her mother had no patience for a plant that couldn't be boiled or canned. There was a single peony bush in the front yard that her brothers routinely drove over with their trucks. Nothing else on the farm could be classified as ornamental, except maybe the brothers, whose main contribution was musical. Today Heath grows masses of flowers and exotic shrubs everywhere around the house, but the vegetable garden is a place I go when I want to be alone.

We seldom warm to an occupation simply because we are told it is good for us. We must discover its goodness for ourselves before we develop any enthusiasm for it. At every farm meeting I attend, someone inevitably comes to the podium to talk about how important it is to educate the urban consumer about how their food is produced. I'm not sure how much anyone south of Highway 7 wants to be educated. Personally, I've never heard anyone talk about a longing to be educated, unless they are a politician back-pedalling from some unfortunate remark they have posted on Twitter. The rest of us would far rather hear a story. And the countryside is full of great stories that often fill the gaps in our understanding of each other.

Ten years ago my eldest daughter, Maddie, picked up stakes and moved to Calgary, following a boy. Her mother and I were a bit glum driving back to the farm after dropping her off at the airport, and I began to talk about how I left home when I was seventeen and ended up on the other side of the world.

"It will be good for her to go to the other side of the country and find out that people live just like we do," I said. "That's what I did, and it made the world seem smaller and more manageable."

I went to Australia in the fall of 1969 and landed in Nanneella South, a rural crossroads in the irrigation country along the Murray River, where I found work milking seventy-five cows for Keith and Margaret Broad. Over the next few months we brought in thousands of square bales of hay and built them into massive stacks covered with tarps. Margaret made me sausages on toast with ketchup every morning after the milking. The school bus drove by the kitchen window and the mailman followed soon after. Keith's mother, Helen, did my laundry on her visits to the farm. On Sunday we all went to a little church in the village with its memorial to the neighbourhood's soldiers from the Boer War and both world wars. On Saturday nights I danced with a pretty schoolteacher at the community hall, to the strains of a trio playing "The Pride of Erin," "The Charmaine Waltz" and all sorts of square dances. I was even asked to give a talk about Canada at a Junior Farmers meeting in the town of Rochester 5 miles away. And at Margaret's kitchen table the conversation ranged over every subject under the sun, as people from unlikely backgrounds laughed and told stories and found common ground.

After five months I moved on, but I came back before the end of my trip to say goodbye. Even in those days I was carrying a tiny portable typewriter and writing bad poetry. I left the typewriter with Margaret to reduce my luggage weight for the flight home.

"Why did you not stay in touch with those people?" asked Heath. I did write to Margaret for a few years, and my dad even went to visit the Broads when the Stratford Festival Company flew to Australia for a tour in 1974. But I eventually lost touch with them.

That night when we got back from the airport I went online and found Keith and Margaret Broad. They had moved into Rochester, and their son Jeffrey had taken over the farm and was now serving on the local irrigation council. There was a phone number for them, and I calculated it would be ten o'clock on a Monday morning their time.

On an impulse I dialled the number.

"Aaaallo?" said a voice.

"Hello, Margaret?"

"Denny ... is that you? Well, come on over and we'll get you fixed up!"

I told her I was in Canada, and she said that was a coincidence because Jeffy was flying to Canada for a wedding. He would come and see me.

"Where is he going?"

"He's going to Edmonton."

I told her that I was actually two time zones east of Edmonton, but that didn't seem to make any difference.

"He flies all over the place. He'll come and see you."

Three weeks later, Jeffy and his wife, Ruth, landed in our kitchen and spent the week with us. His only specific memory of me was the day I left the farm on my motorcycle after a family picnic when he was four years old, but his mother had talked about me many times. Forty years had passed, and she still had my typewriter. I took Jeffy and Ruth to visit dairy farms, and we all spent a night in Niagara Falls together.

In the years since, Jeffy and I have made a point to call each other at Christmas. Four years ago two of his kids, Michael and Katy, came to stay with us and made a connection with my youngest daughter. We all piled in the van and went to Niagara Falls again. Just before the pandemic hit, Hannah, our youngest, was making her own plans to fly to the other side of the world to visit a snake-infested dairy farm on the Murray River. Instead, she had to make her way west to work in the mountains as a camp cook for her uncle who is a horseback outfitter and then north to Grande Prairie to drive a rock truck for the winter. Eventually, she settled near her sister in Calgary to help run a social media business for the food industry, a job that didn't exist when she was going to school. Wherever she lands, she will always be a country girl who can whip up a béchamel sauce or drive a skid-steer, as the occasion requires.

When the children ask me what they should be doing with their lives I give them Carl Jung's advice. He said we should look back to childhood and ask ourselves what it was we did that made time fly. The answer is there somewhere. I had a huge sand plain to play in formed by the spring runoff passing through the culvert under the farm lane a hundred yards from the house. Masses of horsetail grew over that patch of sand every summer, like a miniature white pine forest. I made clearings in the forests and built farms and a village connected by roads and populated it with all the farm animals and vehicles from the toybox. I'm sure you could find some of them still there in the dirt if you dug deep enough. It took me nearly thirty years to recreate that sandbox in my head, but I have been playing contentedly in it ever since. As a fox some days and a hedgehog the next, I have come to understand that deciding what we do with our lives has to be a work of the imagination. That is why I bounce back and forth between the theatre and the farm. You can't take a single step in either place without imagining possibilities. It's terrific exercise and prevents the accumulation of reptiles in the brain. And, perhaps most importantly, I have come to believe that a work of the imagination works best when it engages not only our heads and our hearts, but also the land under our feet.

Acknowledgements

Many of the ideas for these essays germinated in columns I have written for various magazines over the years. *Harrowsmith, Country Guide, Small Farm Canada, In the Hills, On the Bay, Watershed* and *Farmers Forum* have all hosted me for long stretches. Columns are thumbnail sketches that can be moulded into scenes and find their way into a play or a stage show. I also draw from them to entertain after-dinner audiences. Eventually they may find their way into a book. Along the way, as these ideas are teased out, I have been helped by a stable of editors who, in my opinion, never seem to get the credit they deserve for making a writer look good.

First, I would like to thank my editor for *Finding Larkspur*, Meg Taylor, who has now helped me bring four books to publication. I can't imagine trying to do this with anyone else at this point in my life. Peter Gredig was the first magazine editor to coax me into print in 1996 when he was editing *Country Guide*, and I am still firing pages off to him today, trusting in his broad understanding of farm matters. Tom Cruickshank and Yolanda Thornton sustained me through twenty-five years with *Harrowsmith*. For more than ten years, Signe Ball, the force behind *In the Hills* magazine, has been giving my pieces a close read, sharpening my sentences and always seeking clarity, which is all a writer wants in the end. More recently, Tom Henry and Julie Harlow at *Small Farm* and Patrick Meagher at *Farmers Forum* have been instructive, encouraging and fun to write for.

A number of people who are not editors have also contributed to *Finding Larkspur*: Jonathan Pearce, my agent at Westwood Creative Artists and his colleague Chris Casuccio, Ian Bell, Steve McKee, Tony Hendrie, Will Samis, Andrew (Mike) Currie, and all the members of Neil Currie's Driveshed Coffee Club, Rod and Doug Beattie, Rick Archbold, Joe Kertes, Wesley Bates, Ian McLeod, Terry Sheridan,

Dr.Jason Durish, Dr. John Coombs, Susie Meisner, and my brother Art Needles.

And lastly, to Heath, the final reader, always at my back and peering over my shoulder at the same time, an impossible task for anyone but a writer's wife.

With so much assistance, there should be no excuse for error at all. But if a few have slipped through the net, it is no one's fault but my own.

Dan Needles has spent his entire life living and writing about the rural–urban divide. He grew up in farm country in southwestern Ontario and travelled the world working on farms in Canada, England, France and Australia. He studied agricultural economics at university and worked as a journalist, aide and speechwriter to a rural politician and, finally, as an insurance executive until the success of his Wingfield Farm stage plays enabled him to move permanently to the small farm near Georgian Bay that he bought when he was twenty-seven. Since 1988 he has made a living as a writer from that farm.